A Good Name

By Lorraine Davies Knopf

ISBN: 149429818X
ISBN 13: 9781494298180

This story was inspired by a true event. The protagonist, a close friend of the author, has given permission to tell her story. Names of those living have been changed at her request. This book is dedicated to her.

A Good Name is rather to be chosen than great riches,
And loving favor rather than silver and gold.

Proverbs: 22:1

ONE

Just as a light snow began to fall, Betsy and Neil Sanders pulled into a parking spot at New York's La Guardia Airport in their brand new sapphire blue 1960 Thunderbird. Bobby Darin's "Mack the Knife" was playing loudly on the radio. It stopped when the engine was turned off.

"Here we are," Betsy announced.

"Yep. Here we are," said Neil dolefully.

"You should do something about your excess enthusiasm. How many valium did you take anyway?" asked Betsy.

Neil laughed. "Sorry to be such a wet blanket. I'm just not that happy about going."

"I'm not happy at all that you're going. You don't usually take business trips on the weekend. Plus, you never fly. Why are you doing it this time?" Betsy inquired.

"Didn't have a choice. Meeting's tomorrow morning. This was a last minute arrangement."

"This morning we were all set to play bridge with the Rosens tonight."

"Make my apologies. You should go on home now. It's starting to snow again."

"Hey! You're not getting rid of me that easy. I'm going in with you."

"There's really no point in your doing that," protested Neil.

"Point, or not, I'm seeing you off. Let's go."

They made a spectacular couple as they walked into the terminal attracting the attention of other travelers. Betsy, a tall fashion model of Swedish descent, with blonde hair and green eyes, was dressed in well-fitting French jeans and a short ski parka. Neil, a successful New York Lawyer, in a business suit, was hatless. His boyish tousled black hair drew glances from passing women. He pretended not to notice.

When they reached the terminal for Nation Air they were met with wooden sawhorses forming corridors, and makeshift wooden counters. Everything was in disarray. People were crowding, pushing, confused as to where to go.

"What a mess! Betsy exclaimed.

They approached the temporary check-in counter. Neil handed his ticket to the harassed Agent behind the counter.

"What happened?" Neil asked. "Somebody drop a bomb?"

"They're enlarging the terminal," said the Agent as he checked Neil off the passenger list and tore off part of the ticket. "Your flight's going to be delayed about an hour, Mr. Sanders."

"Why? What's wrong?" asked Neil.

"Nothing serious. Just a precaution. Sorry."

"Sorry really makes it," said Neil.

Neil tossed his duffle bag onto the scale to be checked. The Agent put a tag on it and gave Neil the stub. He glanced at the brown leather briefcase and asked, "Anything else, Mr. Sanders?"

"Nope. That's it."

The Agent waved him on, saying, "You'll be boarding from that temporary shed down at the end."

"Oh, for Christ's sake!" Neil exploded.

Betsy looked at him, concerned.

"You seem upset."

"You know me and flying."

They continued walking toward the end of the corridor when Betsy had an idea.

"Why don't I drive you to Penn Station. You can take the midnight train."

"Gets in too late. I have a breakfast meeting with some bankers."

"What's the meeting about anyway? Is it really that important?" asked Betsy.

"I wouldn't want to bore your pretty head with business," said Neil.

"Where will you be staying tonight?"

"I honestly don't know. Some guy named Rodriguez made all the arrangements. He's meeting me. Listen, there's no reason for you to hang around this dismal place. You ought to get home before the snow gets too deep."

"Okay, but I need to get something to eat first. Let's stop at that snack machine."

"You just had dinner!"

"I know, but I'm feeling a little nauseous. Oh good, they have chocolate covered raisins."

Neil laughed and put money in the machine to obtain the item.

"All the symptoms," he said.

"They say the third child is the backbreaker. Think you can you handle it?" she asked.

"Hey, I'm leaving town, Kid. You're on your own," he teased. "Have you seen the doctor yet?"

"No, Dr. Katz retired. Francine recommended one, but I can't get in until next week. I don't need a doctor to tell me I'm pregnant anyway."

"How are Francine and Jerry by the way?" Neil asked. "We haven't seen them for a while."

"She still hasn't forgiven you for representing Jerry when they almost got a divorce."

"Hell, I got him sleeping with her again. She should thank me," Neil said.

"I'll thank you when you're back home sleeping with me."

"Hey, I'll only be gone a couple of days. I'll miss you, too. Come here."

He pulled her toward him with his free arm, the other holding his briefcase. She put her arms around him, tilting her face to his.

"I never could say no to you, Neil...right from the first."

After a long, sensuous goodbye kiss, she put her hands on his shoulders and looked up at him. He looked past her, and caught the eye of a Hispanic man who gave him a quick nod. Neil stiffened, and removing her hands from his shoulders, said, "You should leave now."

"I still wish you'd think about taking the train."

"I'll think about it, and if I decide to, I'll grab a cab, but YOU..."

"I know. Scram."

"Right. I'll call to make sure you got there okay," Neil said.

"I love you."

"I love you, too, Sweetie."

He watched her walk away. She turned and they waved at each other. She continued up the corridor a ways and, turning back again for one last look, saw Neil walk over and sit beside a Latin looking man. She didn't think anything of it, just kept on walking. It would be something she would later remember.

———

The plane's mechanical trouble turned out to be more complicated than originally diagnosed. The Airline did not have another plane available large enough to hold all the passengers so the flight was divided into two smaller planes. The first plane had taken off earlier. Neil was waiting beside the Hispanic man along with other passengers, a little after midnight, when a voice was heard over the loudspeaker:

"Attention, please. The second section of flight 401 to Miami is ready to board. Repeat. This is the second section of flight 401 to Miami. We are sorry for the inconvenience and delay. Please have your boarding passes ready, and thank you for your patience and for flying Nation Air."

As the DC-6B began to taxi toward the runway, the young, slim, attractive stewardess aboard the fight, walked down the aisle checking to see that seat belts were fastened. She approached Neil and the Hispanic man seated in the front row. Neil was sitting by the window with his briefcase on his lap. The stewardess leaned in toward him.

"Sir, that will have to be stored under your seat, or in the overhead bin."

"I know that! Give me a minute."

The other man glanced over at Neil, surprised by his tone, but said nothing.

"God, I hate flying," he muttered.

Again, the stewardess approached with a request.

"Fasten your seat belt, Sir."

"Oh, for Christ's sake!"

Neil fastened his belt, and the pilot's voice was heard over the intercom announcing they were ready for take-off. The plane's engines revved up. Neil closed his eyes, clenched his fists, and held his breath until they were airborne.

———

By the time Betsy reached home the snow had begun in earnest.. She was glad Neil had insisted she leave. She arrived in time to see a Special on TV with Elvis Presley. He had just been released from the Army. She thought Elvis was the sexiest man on earth...next to Neil of course. After the show, she peeked in on the two children and went to bed. She already missed him. She hated it when he had to go out of town.

"Imagine," she thought. "we've been married almost six years and he still excites me as much as he did at the beginning."

They'd met on Valentine's Day. She had been on a booking for Vogue at Ron Rawling's Studio along with another model, Francine Hiller. Francine was an earthy girl from Turtle Creek, Pennsylvania, a coal mining town. The two could not have been more different. Some people wondered at their friendship. It was Francine's spunk that Betsy admired, having a more conventional demeanor herself, typical of women in the 50's. Francine in turn, was drawn to Betsy's genuineness and loyalty.

Betsy remembered Frank Sinatra's "Fly Me to the Moon" was coming over the speaker. The two were wearing Dior gowns, a cobalt blue strapless on Francine with a beaded tulle skirt. Betsy's was a red satin off the shoulder, with side draping.

They twirled and swirled, moving effortlessly from one pose to another. They had worked together often and were able to anticipate what the other was going to do, and complemented each other's poses. They made a striking duo, Betsy with her loose flowing blonde hair, and Francine with a dark pageboy and straight cut bangs. The shoot was going well. Ron, the photographer, was voicing his approval.

"Fabulous! Good move, now you're cooking'. Oh, that's beautiful! Tilt your head a little, Francine. Part your lips more. Betsy, that's great! You two are hot, hot, hot!"

Betsy grinned. "You never give us any strokes, Ron."

"Oh, what I wouldn't give to have this dress," moaned Francine. "This would knock Jerry off his ass."

The two ad execs standing on the sideline in their suits and ties stared raptly at the two models, giving nods of approval. Satisfied he had gotten what he wanted on film, Ron cut off the lights.

"What are you two doing this evening?" he asked the girls.

"Nothing," they both answered at once.

"You're kidding! This is Valentine's Day, and you don't have any plans?"

"Nope," they both answered again.

"Two beautiful girls like you and you have no plans for Valentine's Day. Why don't you come as my guests to the Viennese Opera Ball at the Waldorf? It's one of the top events of the year. No strings. I'll just escort you there and turn you loose."

"You're a sweetheart, Ron," said Francine, "but I don't have a fucking formal."

Betsy rolled her eyes. Would she ever get used to Francine's expletives?

"Not going to take no for an answer," said Ron. "What if you could wear the gowns you have on now?" He turned to the ad men. "Can that be arranged?"

"Oh, Mr. Rawlings, I don't know about that," one of the men sputtered.

"It'll be great publicity to have the gowns actually being worn in public by these beautiful women. There'll be a million celebrities there. I'll even snap some pictures gratis for the newspaper. You can't buy that kind of promotion."

"Well...." said the other ad man. "We'll have to make a phone call."

Francine's eyes lit up. "If I can wear this, I'm on board. How about you, Betsy?"

"Oh, why not?" said Betsy. "I'll have to leave early though. I have a 9:00 o'clock booking in the morning."

———

The Viennese Opera Ball, held each year, was one of the great charity galas benefitting worthy non-profit organizations. That year's at the Waldorf Astoria was benefitting Carnegie Hall.

The palatial ballroom of the Waldorf with its crystal chandeliers, twinkling lights, and velvet draperies was a virtual fantasy. There were arrangements of fresh white roses on every table around the room, and even some in baskets hanging from the ceiling. At one end was a sumptuous buffet table of hors d'oeuvres: brazil nuts rolled in bacon, Swiss pufflets, caviar, lobster rounds, smoked salmon rolls, and more. Some fellow named Dave Brubeck was playing the piano. The men were all in 'white tie' or tuxedos, the woman in beautiful formal gowns, wearing enough jewelry to keep Tiffany in business for a year.

To honor his promise to the ad men, Ron took some photographs of Betsy and Francine conversing with New York's new Mayor, Robert Wagner. Afterwards, Ron cautioned the girls not to spill anything on their dresses and, true to his word, left them to their own devices.

"Well, that was dull," Francine commented.

Betsy was completely awed. She had never seen any place like this, except in the movies. A waiter approached passing out flutes of Veuve Clicquot Champagne. She took one, hoping it would make her feel more at ease. She looked around, excited at being in the company of some of the celebrities she recognized.

"Is that who I think it is? I can't believe this."

"Most of them are assholes," remarked Francine.

"Hey! A synonym, okay?" said Betsy.

"Sorry. I'll watch it," replied Francine, with no intention of doing so. "Oh look, there's Grace Kelly, actually looking sexy in a bitchin' silver lamé gown."

"Um, yes. I think it's a Balenciaga. Who is that handsome man she's talking to?" asked Betsy.

"Neil Sanders. He's nobody."

"What do you mean 'He's nobody?' What does he do?"

"He's a lawyer. Now THAT'S a synonym," said Francine.

Betsy could not help but grin. She looked back at him to see him staring at her. She turned her head, embarrassed, surprised at the flutter in her stomach.

Francine, noticing her reaction, said, "You don't want to meet him. He's a ladies' man. Look, now he's talking to Sky Blue."

Betsy glanced over again to see Neil talking to an attractive redhead.

"I've heard that name. Is she an actress?"

"Model. She's with the Hartford Agency."

"Well, if he's single I guess he's entitled to talk to whomever he wants. He looks nice enough to me."

"Did you ever hear the old saying, don't judge a book by its cover?" asked Francine.

"I once had a friend named Sylvia who said people were like boxes," said Betsy, "you would like to open them up and see what's inside, but you can't."

"That's a very deep thought," said a male voice behind them.

It was Neil Sanders. "Sorry, I just happened to over-hear. Hello Francine, where's your old man?"

"The sonofabitch has a poker game tonight so I decided to have some fun."

"His loss, I'm sure. You look lovely tonight. Who's the lady in red?"

"This is Betsy, sweetheart of the Sigma Chi."

"Hello, Betsy. I'm Neil Sanders." He reached out to take her hand, held it a moment.   .

"Hello. I'm not sweetheart of anything," said Betsy awkwardly.

"Hard to believe. Why aren't you two eating? The food is exceptional."

"I'm afraid of spilling something on this fucking dress," Francine said.

"I was just thinking of trying some," said Betsy. "Champagne on an empty stomach wasn't such a good idea."

"I'll get you a plate," said Neil, "don't go anywhere."

When he had gone, Betsy looked at Francine reproachfully. "I thought you said you'd watch it."

Francine laughed. "If I'm embarrassing you I'll go talk to someone else. I see Dovima talking to Paul Newman. Always wanted to meet him."

She left Betsy standing there alone, but she was immediately joined by a couple of admiring males. One reached out his hand and said, "I don't believe we've met. My name is Jack..."

Betsy interrupted, taking his hand, "I know who you are, Senator Kennedy. I saw you on Meet the Press. Very pleased to meet you. I'm Betsy Johnson."

"Are you interested in politics?" he asked.

"Not usually," Betsy answered, "but I was very impressed with what you said about how you think France should promote the independence of Indochina."

"Sounds like you're a Democrat."

"I have to confess I voted for General Eisenhower. But if you run for President, I will definitely vote for you."

"I'd love to be President, if only I didn't have to be a politician in the process," he said.

The other man also reached out to shake hands, and said, "Hi, I'm Peter Lawford, and may I say that is a beautiful dress you're wearing."

"Thank you," Betsy replied. "I wish I could take credit for designing it."

Neil returned with a plate of food and a possessive attitude, giving the impression that she was his date, The other men got the message.

"Nice to have met you," Kennedy said with a smile, the two withdrawing to explore new territory.

"Where's Francine?" Neil asked.

"She's miffed because I asked her to tone down her language. She thinks I'm a Pollyanna."

"She does have a mouth," remarked Neil.

"I take it you and Francine have met before."

"We're old acquaintances. I did some legal work for her husband, Jerry. How did you two meet?"

"We're with the same agency and we've modeled together many times. I like her."

"I guessed that you were a model. You're the most beautiful woman here. In fact you're out-shining the debutantes."

Betsy laughed. "You don't expect me to fall for a line like that, do you? I saw you talking to Grace Kelly."

"She's an iceberg."

"Are you confessing you couldn't melt her?"

"I'd like to get to know you better, Betsy. What do you say we get out of here at a decent hour and go for a ride through Central Park in one of those horse drawn carriages. Have you ever done that?"

"No, I haven't even seen a horse since I left Kansas."

"Well, you're about to see one in a few minutes right here," he said.

"What are you talking about?" asked Betsy.

"Just watch," said Neil, "it's a tradition."

Sure enough, a string quartet struck up a Viennese waltz, and a splendid white Viennese Lipizzaner stallion was escorted through the main hallway. Everyone applauded. The magnificent animal pranced across the room with fluid movements, demonstrating the knee action and delicate placing of the feet for which they are so famous. In the center of the room it performed a pirouette, curtsied, and exited with a stately vertical carriage of the head. The evening had now officially begun. To Betsy it felt like wonderland.

"That ride in the carriage is really looking good now," she said.

"Let's do it then. You can tell me all about Kansas. I've never met anyone from Kansas before. Is that in the United States?"

As they were walking out of the hotel later, Betsy realized she couldn't go in a horse drawn carriage in that Dior gown.

"Would you mind terribly if I stop and change first?" she asked when they got in a cab.

"Not at all. Where do you live?"

Betsy leaned forward and said to the driver, "The Barbizon Hotel please, Lexington and 59th."

Neil leaned back and hit his head with his fist. "Don't tell me you live at the Barbizon!"

Betsy raised her eyebrows. "What's wrong with the Barbizon?"

"No men allowed past the lobby."

"You...didn't think I was...inviting you up...did you?"

"Oh no, of course not," he lied, "it's just too overly protective for my taste."

"That's what I like about it," she retorted.

The Barbizon, a hotel for women only, had the reputation of being a place where wealthy parents sent their daughters to be sure they would be living where men couldn't get at them. Most of the girls were going to posh secretarial schools like Katherine Gibbs, where they had to wear hats, stockings and white gloves. Though it was pricey, the rooms were tiny, with a small single bed, and many had to share a bath.

—

It was very romantic trotting through the park all bundled up under a big fur blanket. Neil was the perfect gentleman and put up a good pretense of being interested in Kansas. Afterwards they went to the Carnegie Deli on Seventh Avenue to top off the evening with their famous New York cheesecake.

"When did you start modeling?" asked Neil.

"About a year ago. I came to New York by winning a magazine essay contest when I was a student at Knox."

"I'm impressed," Neil interrupted, "that's a very good liberal arts college What was your essay about?"

"It was about fashion.   Several other girls from around the country and I were invited to work at the magazine here for a month. We were given passes to fashion shows, hair stylings at expensive salons, and such. Then, at the end of the month I was having a farewell lunch at the Stork Club with one of the girls..."

Neil interrupted, "Oh, the Stork Club. One of my favorite places."

"Mine, too. We girls go there for lunch often. Sherman Billingsly always gives us free perfume," she smiled broadly.

"Yes, he likes to have the models come in. It's good for business. But, as you were saying..."

"I was really sad about leaving. I'd completely fallen in love with New York. Then, while we were eating, a woman from a nearby table came over and gave me her card...this must be boring to you."

"Not at all," said Neil. "Why would you say that?"

"You're looking at me funny."

"I'm fascinated by that dimple in your cheek when you smile. You just said a woman gave you her card. What was it?"

"She said if I was interested she'd like to sign me up with her model agency. I put the card in the ashtray. I had no desire to be a model. My friend was aghast. She said, 'Do you know how much models make an hour?' I said, 'No' and she said, 'They make twenty dollars an hour.' I was floored. Twenty dollars an hour! That was a fortune to me at that time. I thought, this could be my ticket to stay here and go to design school, which was my dream. So, I went for an interview and became a model. End of story."

"And you're making twenty dollars an hour."

"No, my fee is sixty now."

"Wow! And, you get to wear gorgeous gowns like the one you had on tonight. It sounds like a very glamorous business."

"Not always," said Betsy. "I remember a time early on when I was sent to the garment center for a fitting. Have you ever been to New York's garment center?"

"Can't say that I have. What's it like?" asked Neil.

"It's awful! I went into this huge room. The room was wall to wall Puerto Rican women all sewing furiously at little foot peddle machines. I'd never seen anything like it. It was stifling hot and there was no air. I walked through the room to where there was standing the meanest looking, most intimidating man you could imagine. He handed me a dress on a hanger and said, 'Put it on.' I looked around and asked, 'Where is the dressing room?' He leaned into my face and said in a very loud voice, 'Who do you think you are, the Virgin Mary?'"

"So, did you put it on?" asked Neil.

"Certainly not! We just stood there, eye to eye. Suddenly I realized all the sewing machines had stopped. There was total quiet. Then, somewhere two little hands started to clap. The whole room erupted with wild applause. He turned away from me and told a male employee to go get a roll of fabric that was in the corner. They draped the fabric over some overhead pipes and hung a mirror on a pillar for a makeshift dressing room. As I was standing there while an elderly woman was pinning the dress, all I could think of was, Betsy, you're not in Kansas anymore."

Betsy's original intention to make an early night of it was forgotten. She did not get back to the Barbizon until two-thirty in the morning, way past the hotel's curfew. To the consternation of the hotel night clerk, Neil took Betsy in his arms and planted a big kiss on her right in the middle of the lobby. She offered no resistance.

The next day a shock of flowers arrived at the hotel for Betsy. There were lilies and roses and zinnias and small yellow sunflowers, wrapped in green florist paper. They were from Neil, of course, and included an invitation for dinner that evening at the Viennese Lantern, a restaurant popular with New Yorkers as an after theater rendezvous, because of its romantic atmosphere featuring roaming violinists.

TWO

One month and three days after they met, Betsy and Neil were nestled in a booth at Spumoni's, a small Italian restaurant on Third Avenue with a casual atmosphere. The scent of garlic and herbs permeated the room. Dean Martin was crooning "Volare" over the sound system.

"Why are we in an Italian restaurant on St. Patrick's Day instead of an Irish one?" Betsy asked.

"Because I hate green beer," Neil answered.

"The desk clerks at the hotel were dressed like leprechauns today," said Betsy. "It was cute."

"Aren't you getting tired of living at the Barbizon?" asked Neil.

"I am. Business has been so good I've been thinking about getting an apartment."

"Why don't you move in with me?" he asked.

A waiter came to the table with bread and a saucer of olive oil.

"Are you ready to order?" the waiter asked.

"Not yet." Neil answered. "Bring us a bottle of your best Chianti."

"Right away sir."

The waiter departed. Neil addressed Betsy again.

"Well?"

"I hear their lasagna is great."

"You haven't answered my question."

"I can't do that."

"You can't answer my question or you can't move in with me?"

"Both."

"Betsy, we've been together every night since we met. I want more than a goodnight kiss in the hotel lobby, even though I do love upsetting that night clerk. I'm crazy about you."

The waiter brought the wine and two glasses. He poured for them. Betsy took a sip.

"Um, this is good."

"You're leaving me hanging."

"You may not understand, and I don't know how to explain."

"Try," he said, taking a big swallow of wine.

The waiter returned and asked, "Are you ready to order?"

"Oh for God's sake, yes, two salads and two lasagnas." He looked at Betsy, "Okay?"

"Sounds perfect."

Neil pressed her once more.

"I'm waiting," he said, impatiently.

"May I be completely honest?"

"Of course. I can't imagine you being otherwise." He took a sip of wine.

"I can't meet your expectations."

"What expectations? I don't get it," he said, bewildered.

"I'm aware that you've had plenty of sexual experience and would expect that if I moved in with you. I don't intend to have sex until I'm married. I know that sounds old-fashioned, but that's the way I am."

"You mean you've never..."

"Never."

He scratched his head and took another swallow of wine, finishing the glass. He poured another for himself.

"I don't know what to say. I hadn't thought that far ahead."

She laughed.

"Neil, I'm not proposing."

"I should hope not, that's my job. So what do you say?"

"About what?"

"Will you marry me?"

"If it wasn't so cliché I'd say, 'Oh, this is so sudden'," Betsy laughed. "Why don't you ask me another time when you haven't had any wine."

"I'll do that. Meet me in front of Tiffany's at 11:00 in the morning."

"Can't. I have a booking from 10:00 to 12:00."

"Oh, for Christ's sake! You're killing me! Meet me at 12:30 then."

"Shouldn't you at least introduce me to your mother first?"

"I don't want to introduce you to my mother...ever," he said.

"Why? Won't she like me?"

"No, and you won't like her either."

"I find that hard to believe."

"You'll see."

———

"Good evening, Mr. Sanders," greeted the doorman at the swanky apartment house on Sutton Place South, which was the residence of Renata Sanders, Neil's mother. Betsy was wearing a simple black dress, and a single strand of pearls, determined to make a good impression.

"Evening to you, George," replied Neil.

They took the elevator to the 8th floor and rang the bell. The door was answered by a Latina maid in uniform.

"Good evening, Mr. Sanders. Nice to see you," said the maid.

"Same here, Alicia, this is Miss Johnson, my fiancée."

"Hello," said Alicia, nodding. "Your mother will be out in a few minutes, please make yourselves comfortable." She retired to the kitchen.

They sat on the sofa together. Betsy took stock of the room. It was tastefully decorated with expensive antique furniture and paintings by minor Impressionists. She knew a bit about art, and was pretty sure that was a Suzanne Eisendieck above the fireplace. There was also a spectacular view of the East River.

She was totally unprepared for the austere woman who swept dramatically into the living room, wearing a long black skirt and a silvery-grey silk blouse that matched her hair.

"Where have you been? I've been calling and calling?" were her first words. She did not even glance at Betsy.

"I've been busy," said Neil. "Mother, I'd like you to meet Betsy Johnson, the girl I'm going to marry."

Betsy started to put her hand out but withdrew it as Renata turned her back and walked over to the wet bar at the end of the living room.

"What would you like to drink before dinner, Neil? I'm having a gin and tonic."

"Sounds good to me," Neil said. "What about you, Betsy?"

"Just plain soda for me."

Renata put ice cubes in some glasses, confirming,

"Two gin and tonics and one plain." The word 'plain' was said with emphasis. "Now. tell me, Neil, what has been keeping you too busy to return your mother's phone calls?"

"Heavy client load right now, and of course I've been spending every moment I could with my fiancée. Do I smell cooking? I thought we were going out."

"I thought it would be more appropriate if we ate in tonight. Alicia's made a coc au vin."

"Coc au vin," Betsy said with enthusiasm. "It's one of my favorite dishes."

"Really."

"Yes, I make it with Burgundy."

"Burgundy has so much sugar," Renata made a face, "Oh, by the way, Neil, I got us two tickets for 'Carousel' next Saturday night. We'll have dinner at Sardi's first."

"I'll have to let you know about that, Mother."

"No excuses, they cost a fortune and they're non-refundable."

Alicia announced that dinner was ready by ringing a little bell.

"Saved by the bell," said Neil.

Renata took Neil's arm as they entered the dining room where she took her place at the head of the table.

"Pour the wine, would you, Neil?"

Neil did as instructed. The tension in the room was palpable. No one spoke as Alicia entered with the first course, oeufs en gelée.

"The Lewins are trying to talk me into buying a condominium on Miami Beach," Renata said, breaking the silence. "There's one available right next to theirs."

"Oh, that sounds wonderful," Betsy said. "I love the beach."

"Where did you go to the beach?" asked Neil. "Not in Kansas for sure."

"Francine and Jerry took me to Coney Island. I loved it!"

"Of course you would," Renata said. "By the way, Neil, I'm thinking of having the living room re-painted. What do you think of Wedgewood blue?"

"Oh, Neil, that would go perfectly with that painting over the fireplace," Betsy exclaimed.

Renata ignored her as if she did not exist. After an uncomfortable pause, Neil tried to smooth things over.

"That's an Eisendieck," he said. "It's been in the family for years."

"I thought it was," said Betsy, "I've admired other works of hers..."   .

"Rabbi Newman has asked me to help with the UJA fund raising affair for a hospital in Israel," Renata interrupted. "I don't know how I always get roped into these things. I'll need your help, Neil."

"I'll do what I can, Mother," Neil replied.

Betsy gave up trying and just sat quietly while Renata gossiped on and on to Neil throughout the dinner about various people at her Temple, whose daughter was getting married, who'd had a face lift, who'd gotten a divorce, as if Betsy were invisible. It was so stunningly obvious. She was actually relieved that she didn't have to participate. She watched as Neil stoically bolted his food and drank several glasses of wine. She could see he was embarrassed, and her heart went out to him, understanding now why he had not wanted to introduce her to his mother. This woman was so foreign to her. Never in her life had she met anyone like her. She wondered if Renata had always been this way. It was disappointing that Neil didn't stand up to her more. Maybe she had been different when Neil's dad was alive. Neil spoke so highly of him.

After what seemed like an eternity to Betsy, Neil announced they should leave because he had an early meeting the next day.

"Oh, but you haven't had dessert," said Renata, "Alicia made your favorite...tarte tatin. I know you can't resist that."

Renata rang the little bell at the side of her plate. Alicia appeared instantly.

"We'll have dessert now, Alicia, and then we'll have coffee in the living room."

"Skip the coffee. I just told you I have to get up early," said Neil irritably.

"Perhaps Betty would like some."

"It's Betsy, Mother. Her name is Betsy."

———

They left right after dessert. When they exited the building, Betsy turned to Neil and said, "That woman is the rudest person I ever met in my life. I'm sorry. I shouldn't be criticizing your mother. I didn't expect her to hug me or anything, but she didn't even look at me, much less talk to me, or make any acknowledgment of our engagement. I felt like she doesn't think I'm good enough for you."

"I did warn you when you said you wanted to meet her."

"I thought you were exaggerating. Is it because I'm not Jewish?"

"That may have something to do with it, but mostly it's because I love you."

"Neil, she's never going to accept me as a daughter-in-law."

"I wish I could say you're wrong, but you're probably right. God, I wish my father were still alive. He'd have loved you."

"She's going to be my children's grandmother."

"Don't worry. Renata doesn't do children. I promise you won't have any problems there."

———

When Betsy's first generation Swedish parents were told of the engagement they were taken by surprise, and concerned that things were moving too fast. They urged a long engagement. Betsy gave them until June to arrange for a Church wedding in Kansas. She was serious about remaining a virgin until marriage, but their passion could not wait. So without telling anyone except Francine and Jerry, who stood up with them, they were quietly married in April by a Judge in New York, all the while keeping plans to have a formal wedding two months later in Betsy's home town church. Betsy wore a light blue cashmere suit for the Civil ceremony and they all went to the Stork Club for dinner afterwards. Sherman Billingsly sent over a bottle of champagne when he learned they were newlyweds. They spent their wedding night at the Plaza Hotel. Neil was an expert and considerate lover. He made sure Betsy's first sexual experience was as exciting and loving as it could possibly be.

Betsy flew to Kansas a week early for the Church wedding to have some time with her family and help with final plans. Neil drove out. It was then that Betsy first learned how much Neil hated flying. They drove to Memphis for their honeymoon at the Peabody Hotel. Betsy was thrilled by the "March of the ducks" that occurred each morning at 11:00 o'clock. Exactly on the hour, the lobby elevator doors open, and a parade of white ducks walk across the red carpet and jump into a fountain that is in the middle of the lobby. Unfortunately, there was an embarrassing incident involving the fountain. Betsy was leaning over, looking into it, when she suddenly became dizzy and almost vomited into the fountain.

"It was the raw oysters, "Neil said. "I knew you shouldn't have eaten them! Who serves raw oysters in the month of June anyway? Let's get you upstairs, and I'm going to have a talk with the manager."

"Oh, Neil, don't make a fuss. It's my own fault. I would like to go lie down though."

When Neil made his complaint, the manager insisted it could not possibly have been the oysters because they were flown in fresh from Alaska each day. He suggested having the hotel doctor see her. The doctor came to their room and, after asking a few questions, quickly solved the problem. Betsy was two months pregnant!

There was an awkward explanation to make to her parents when their first child arrived only seven months after the nuptials. Renata, of course, did not attend the wedding, although she did send a sizable monetary gift. When their son was born, Neil told Betsy that his mother had requested they name him after a deceased relative, which was the Jewish tradition. He asked if that was okay with her.

"My grandfather's name was Sven. How about that?" asked Betsy.

"Sven Sanders. Umm, that has a nice ring to it," said Neil, with a devilish smile.

"What kind of name is that for a Jewish boy?" Neil's mother, Renata, had screamed when she learned of the name.

Aside from interferences by her mother-in-law, Betsy considered her marriage ideal. Neil was doing well financially and they had purchased a spacious Tudor-style home in Stamford, Connecticut. They enjoyed ski trips in Vermont in the winter, and sailing on Long Island Sound, in their 'Sunfish' on summer weekends. A little girl, Ana, short for Anastasia, Neil's deceased grandmother, was born three years after Sven's birth.

Betsy continued to be in demand as a model, even with taking time off for the births of the children. They had acquired a warm-hearted, live–in Nanny from Jamaica named Lillian, to free her for bookings. Neil's career as a corporate lawyer also seemed to be on the rise, requiring him to take occasional trips out of town, which Betsy did not like, but adjusted to. They had good friends, especially next door neighbors, Fred and Elise Rosen, with whom they played bridge and shared casserole dinners on occasion. They had two beautiful children, security, good health, and her parents had moved from Kansas to be near. All else, aside from those trips, it was, for Betsy, a picture perfect marriage.

THREE

Betsy was sleeping soundly at 6:00 A.M. when the phone rang. She groped for it, not really awake, catching it on the third ring. The ringing had awakened Ana in the nursery next door, who began to cry.

"Hello."

"Mrs. Sanders?"

"Yes, who is this?"

"My name is Carl Rodriguez. I was supposed to meet your husband in Miami."

"The plane was late leaving," she mumbled.

"Do you know for sure he was on it?"

"Yes, I took him to the airport."

"Mrs. Sanders...."

"Neil called after I was in bed and said they were dividing the flight into two smaller planes and probably wouldn't take off until after midnight."

"I know that. One plane has arrived. The other's been reported lost."

"Lost?"

She tried to say more but no sound would come out. Meanwhile Ana's cries had gotten louder. Was something the matter? she worried. Mr. Rodriguez tried to get her attention again.

"Mrs. Sanders...are you there?"

Betsy was torn between attending to the baby, or staying on the phone. She couldn't comprehend what the man was saying. His words were not registering. Ana's cries were distracting her.

"Yes...I'm sorry...the baby...can you hold on?"

"Is it possible your husband was not on that plane?"

"We talked about his taking the train. I don't know..."

A loud click indicated the caller had hung up.

"Hello...hello..."

Stunned, she hung up the phone and jumped out of bed to get Ana whose crying had increased in volume. Thankfully Sven had not been awakened by Ana's crying. Just like Neil, she thought, he could sleep through anything. She quickly changed her and went downstairs to the kitchen. She put the child in her highchair, turned on the radio, and froze as she heard:

"...exploded and crashed over North Carolina. No survivors have been reported. The craft was one of two substituted for a larger 707 aircraft pulled out of service. The list of passengers will not..."

She turned off the radio, and with shaking hands, poured cheerios onto the highchair tray to keep Ana occupied while she prepared breakfast. She chattered to the child in a nervous manner, denying to herself what she knew deep inside but couldn't face.

"I'll bet Daddy decided to take the train. I told him he should do that, and he said he might. He'll call us soon. I know he will."

The wall phone rang, startling her. She snatched it off the hook.

"Neil?" But it wasn't Neil. It was a representative of Nation Air informing her of the crash.

The life drained out of her as she listened. Shock waves went through her body. She heard the words, but they didn't make sense. And where was that jackhammer noise coming from? A heartbeat can't be that loud.

"Oh, no...oh, no...no! Everybody? Maybe there's a chance, are you certain he was on the plane...oh, my God...yes, please let me know."

She hung up the phone, her knees turning to jelly, and with a wail, she slid down against the wall to the floor.

———

At the home of Aaron and Sarah Ross, the two were having breakfast in the kitchen, still in their pajamas and robes, at 6:30 am. Aaron, an Attorney, was also a long-time friend of Neil's family. They had been listening to the radio about the Nation Air plane crash. The phone rang. Aaron picked it up, muttering "Who the heck is calling at this hour?" It was Betsy Sanders. From the expression on his face as he listened, Sarah could see that he was appalled by what he was hearing. He covered the mouth piece with his hand and spoke to her.

"Neil Sanders was on that plane that crashed last night."

Sarah gasped and covered her mouth in horror. She stared at her husband. Aaron was speaking to Betsy on the phone.

"Would you like me to call Neil's mother?...Yes, of course, I'll be there as soon as I can."

Aaron hung up the phone in shock, and looked at his wife.

"I have to go over there."

Sarah, eyes brimming with tears, said, "You'd better call Renata first, before she hears it on the radio."

"That isn't going to be easy. Damn! Planes don't just explode!"

———

The early morning sun was sparkling on the new snow as Aaron arrived at the Sanders home just as the Reverend Bill Brooks, ex-football player in his early 40's, pulled up in his Jeep. They reached the door together, introduced themselves to each other, and rang the doorbell.

The door was opened by Betsy's mother, Katie Johnson, still attractive at fifty, an older version of Betsy. The look on her face said it all. As the two men entered the house, Betsy's father, Mr. Johnson, a soft-spoken, self-made man, could be heard giving obituary information to the newspaper on the telephone.

"He was thirty-two, graduated from Harvard Law. His father was Adam Sanders, former District Attorney. He died a few years ago...I don't know...Yes, two, a boy and a girl...No, there haven't been any arrangements made yet. I imagine it'll be at the Redeemer Lutheran. That's my daughter's Church...we'll let you know...yes, goodbye."

Aaron and Bill each embraced Katie and asked how Betsy was doing. Katie replied that the hardest part was telling the children. They proceeded from the entrance way further into the living room and were confronted by the saddest sight either had ever seen.

Betsy was seated on the sofa, clutching the children to her. Her face had been ravaged by crying. Ana with her thumb in her mouth and Sven's face buried in Betsy's breast. Bill quickly crossed the room and knelt before the three, encircling them protectively with his arms.

Sven raised his head and looked directly into the eyes of Bill Brooks as he spoke.

"Do you know where my daddy is?" he asked.

An agonized look crossed Betsy's face as Bill answered.

"Yes, Sven, your daddy is in Heaven."

"If we could find him and take him to a hospital, he wouldn't be dead," Sven stated with conviction.

Bill pulled Sven to him and cradled him in his arms. Betsy then asked her mother to take the children away so she could talk with Bill. The grandparents took the children from her to go upstairs. Aaron had seated himself unobtrusively in a chair near the sofa, not wanting to intrude, but wanting to be there. Bill sat on the sofa beside Betsy and took her hand.

"I don't know how to explain it to him," she said.

"I'll talk to him later," Bill said.

"Thank you. I appreciate that."

They sat a few seconds in silence. Then Bill asked Betsy if she felt like talking.

"I don't know what I feel. I feel like I'm sleepwalking. I just can't believe it. I know it, but I can't believe it," Betsy uttered. "Just yesterday afternoon he and Sven were having fun down in the basement playing with the model train set. Then we had an early dinner with the kids because he had to leave on that business trip. He never flies. I tried to get him to take the train. Oh, God, how could this happen?"

"There are some questions that can't be answered," said Bill.

"Bill, you told Sven his daddy is in Heaven. Do you really believe that?" asked Betsy.

"I believe that's between Neil and God," replied Bill.

"Will you give him a Christian burial, even though he never officially joined the Church?"

"Of course, if you think that's what he'd have wanted.'

"I do. He admired you so much, and remember how he enjoyed teaching that Old Testament lesson in the Sunday school class?"

Aaron was thunderstruck. He almost stuttered as he jumped from the chair to speak.

"Betsy, I wasn't aware...I just assumed..."

"Oh Aaron, I'm sorry. I never even said hello," said Betsy. "Did you meet Bill?"

Bill interrupted, concerned, "Aaron, what were you trying to say?"

"When I called Renata, she said to make arrangements to have him buried in the Jewish cemetery."

"No! She can't do that!" Betsy cried.

"I didn't realize..."

"She was always trying to run his life...you don't know..."

She was beginning to hyper-ventilate. Bill made an effort to calm her.

"I'm sure this can be resolved," he said.

Betsy refused to calm down. She was quivering with rage.

"They haven't even found him yet, and already she's trying to take over!"

"What do you mean they haven't found him," asked Bill in astonishment.

"I mean they haven't found him! Everyone else is accounted for." Her voice broke. "He's lying dead somewhere and no one even knows where he is."

A look passed between Bill and Aaron. Both were unnerved by this information.

FOUR

At the wreckage site in North Carolina the airplane lay strewn about the ground, covering a vast area. It had been roped off with yellow tape in an unsuccessful effort to keep the gawkers out. County Sheriff's men and members of the National Guard were working to collect parts of the plane, later to be reassembled. The Coroner's men were attending to the gruesome task of picking up bodies and zipping them up in black plastic sacks as a light rain was falling.

Curiosity seekers had gathered like vultures, bringing their cameras. It was bitter cold, and people were bundled up in hunting jackets or sweaters. A small black Mercedes with 1960 Florida license plates and tinted windows crept up to the outer perimeter of the crowd. It looked out of place among the jeeps, vans and pickups. The two men who exited looked out of place, too. They looked Latin, with olive complexions and black moustaches. They were dressed in expensive trench coats and hats. They made their way through the crowd up to the barrier, surveying the wreckage.

———

Fred Rosen, the Sanders' next door neighbor, was a stock broker. He took an early morning commuter train into Manhattan every day. As was his custom, he sat with his three buddies, Charlie, Al and Joe, in facing seats with a table between them to play cards during the hour ride. Joe was also a stock broker, Charlie and Al were in advertising. The four of them took the same train daily back and forth to the city. They were "train buddies" and did not socialize otherwise. Instead of playing cards that particular day, however, they, and everyone else on the train, were reading the New York Times. The headlines read:

"34 ON MIAMI-BOUND PLANE KILLED IN CAROLINA CRASH. EXPLOSION HEARD SHORTLY BEFORE AIRLINER FROM NEW YORK PLUNGED"

There was also a photograph of the horribly mangled airplane.

"My next door neighbor was on that plane," said Fred to the astonishment of the others.

"No shit!" exclaimed Charlie.

"Yeah, Neil Sanders. He was a lawyer."

"The guy they haven't found yet?" asked Al.

"Hey, wasn't he married to that Swedish-looking model?" Charlie interjected.

"Yeah, that's him. She and my wife are good friends. She's a really nice gal."

"Any kids?"

"Two, boy and a girl."

"Damn! That's a shame," said Joe. "I hope he had some insurance at least."

"He may not have," Fred answered. "He was such a cocky bastard he probably thought he was immortal."

The others looked at him in surprise.

"I take it he wasn't one of your favorite people," Joe commented.

"I never had a problem with him. It's just that he was too full of himself. I Never understood how he captured a classy lady like Betsy."

"Maybe he had hidden assets," said Charlie suggestively.

———

The Johnsons were spending the night with Betsy. It was a cozy scene with them all sitting in front of the fireplace, Mr. Johnson smoking a pipe and Katie knitting. Betsy sitting on the hearth, hunched, her back to the fire. Katie broke the silence.

"I never thought I'd see the day you'd give in to Renata," she said.

"I didn't give in to Renata. I gave in to Bill Brooks. He said it's all Renata's got left."

"Yes, it was the right decision. You know, we could have a Christian service here at the house beforehand, if you'd like," Katie suggested.

"Bill said I'm young, and would probably marry again someday."

"That's true," Katie allowed.

"No, I can't imagine being with someone else. Neil and I both poured so much of ourselves into making our marriage work," said Betsy.

"You make it sound like a project. Was it necessary to work so hard?" asked Katie.

"Not everybody goes together like mashed potatoes the way you two do. We were more like hot chili and cornbread. I was certainly 'corn bred.'" Betsy laughed a little at her own pun.

"And he was full of beans," Mr. Johnson added. Then, "I'm sorry, sugar. I didn't mean anything by that. He took good care of you, and that makes him okay in my book."

Betsy moved over to sit on the floor beside him. "It's all right, Dad. I've always known you two weren't crazy about Neil."

"That's not true!" Katie protested, "We were just concerned at first because it all happened so fast. You hardly knew him."

"But we knew it was right from the beginning. We were always so totally honest with each ..." She suddenly doubled over, grimacing in pain.

"What's wrong!" Both parents asked anxiously.

"Just a cramp...I'm okay."

"I don't like the sound of that," said Katie. "Have you seen the doctor yet?"

"Now when have I had time, Mother? I'll go soon. Don't worry."

"I can't help but worry. You've been under a terrible strain. Why don't you go on up to bed now?"

"Maybe I will. I do feel kind of shaky," admitted Betsy.

Mr. Johnson spoke up, too. "This is no time to get sick."

Betsy laughed ironically. "Right, Dad. No time."

She rose and kissed both parents goodnight.

She went up to the bedroom and climbed into 'her' side of the bed. When she turned off the bedside lamp, the room was bathed in soft moonlight coming through the window. She lay there, staring at the shadows on the ceiling and thoughts of Neil flooded over her. His smile, his mischievous eyes, that coal black hair that she loved to tousle...Her body was aching for him. She reached over to Neil's side of the bed, grabbing his pillow, and curled up into a fetal position. She hugged the pillow to her body and cried into it until there were no tears left.

FIVE

A few days later, in the early A.M. two fishermen were casting their lines into the mist on the Cape Fear River in North Carolina. One of them, Leroy, was complaining about everything.

"Dog it, it's cold!" he lamented.

His companion, Andy, was beginning to lose patience with him.

"Stop whining," Andy said, "you're getting on my nerves."

Leroy reached into the cooler.

"I'm hungry, whatcha got in here?"

"Get your cotton-pickin' hands outta there," scolded Andy, "did you come to fish or eat?"

"Well...Hell," said Leroy, and cast his line out.

"Don't cast toward the bank, you idiot!" warned Andy. Leroy began to reel in his line, and it met with resistance. "Dad gum it," he complained, "I hit a snag."

"I told you not to cast toward the bank," Andy exhorted, "you might just as well cut your line. You'll never get loose."

"It's moving," Leroy said, "I think I can pull it in."

"You're worse'n a woman, Leroy. You're gonna snap your rod. Point it down at least."

Leroy pointed his rod down toward the water and continued to reel in whatever was on the end of his line. Andy leaned over, peering into the water.

"Okay, I see it. It's something shiny," he said as he reached out and retrieved a distorted Airline window frame from the water.

"Leroy, you know what this looks like to me? It might be part of that plane that crashed."

They looked at each other in amazement. Leroy excitedly suggested they go ashore and see if they could find something else. Andy pulled up the small mushroom-shaped anchor as Leroy started rowing toward shore in the direction he had cast. Nearing the river-bank they spotted an eight foot section of the wall of a plane lying half in the water. As they got closer, the mist became less dense, and a twisted airplane seat could be seen up on the bank. They brought the boat to the edge and Leroy jumped out, suddenly energized.

"I see a seat up there. Maybe we'll get lucky and find a pocketbook or something."

"We're taking in anything you find," admonished Andy.

Leroy was off in a flash, heading up the bank.

"Watch out for cottonmouths," Andy called out, but Leroy had already disappeared. Andy stepped out of the boat, and was in the process of securing it to a fallen tree with a short line when Leroy came thrashing back through the weeds, pale and shaken.

"I just found something we're sure as hell not taking in!"

———

Aaron and Sarah were still asleep when the phone rang. Aaron answered it on the second ring and swung his feet to the floor. He responded to the caller, "Yes, of course. I'll take the first flight available."

"What is it?" Sarah asked, turning on a bedside lamp.

"They found Neil...twenty miles away from the crash site."

"Why do you have to go down there?" she asked.

"To identify the body. You wouldn't want Betsy to do that."

———

When Aaron went into the refrigerator-cold room of the morgue in North Carolina he was met with the sight of Neil's body on a stainless steel table, covered with a sheet. A representative from Nation Air, Wally Cooper, was also there. The coroner, wearing a surgical gown, cap and surgical gloves stood by the table. All were wearing surgical masks. As the coroner lifted the sheet from the mutilated, decomposing body, Aaron gasped and turned away. He could feel his heart rate increasing.

"We're going to need a positive ID," the coroner said.

Aaron steeled himself. He forced himself to give the corpse's grotesquely twisted head closer scrutiny. Then he turned away again, feeling faint.

"Yes...it's him. It's Neil Sanders," he choked out.

Later, when Aaron and Wally exited the building, Aaron leaned against the wall and exhaled as if he had been holding his breath. Wally offered him a cigarette, which he waved away.

"I haven't smoked in five years," Aaron said.

Wally shrugged and lit one for himself. Aaron changed his mind.

"I think I will have one. Maybe it'll kill the stench," he said.

Wally gave him a cigarette and lit it for him. He watched as Aaron took a long draw.

"I guess you haven't had to identify too many bodies," Wally commented.

"Not in that condition."

"Don't you think it's strange he was found twenty miles from the main crash site?"

"Somewhat."

"We're pretty sure the crash was caused by a bomb. Judging from the body, Sanders must have been practically sitting on it."

Aaron's face darkened. He threw down his cigarette and ground it out with his foot.

"I know what you're getting at, and let me tell you... I've known Neil Sanders a long time. He wouldn't."

"That's your opinion."

"And all you've got is an opinion. If I read one line about that in the newspaper, I'll slap a slander suit on you."

This did not appear to faze Wally in the slightest. He glanced at his watch and sauntered off.

"Well...I'll see you back in New York."

SIX

Betsy's next door neighbor and friend, Elise Rosen, had been extremely supportive all throughout since the terrible ordeal began. On that particular afternoon she appeared, bearing dinner for the family.

"It's nothing fancy," she modestly stated, "shepherd's pie. I think the kids will like it."

"Of course they will, and so will I," said Betsy gratefully. "I can't thank you enough for all you've done."

"What? I haven't done anything," said Elise.

"You've held me together. That's what you've done." Betsy gave her a big hug.

"What are friends for? By the way, how is Sven doing? Has Bill Brooks been talking to him?" Elise asked.

"Yes, but I'm having a real problem. He won't go to his pre-school. He's got a birthday coming up next month, Maybe I'll get him a puppy."

"I know a very good child psychologist if you decide to go that route. She's quite expensive though," said Elise.

"If it would help, it's worth whatever it costs," Betsy answered.

At that moment the doorbell rang, and they both went to the front door. The door opened to a young, brash, local reporter.

"I'm from the 'Town Crier' Mrs. Sanders. I'd like to ask you couple of questions if I may," he said.

"I thought your paper had all the information," Betsy replied.

"Senator McKinsey from Massachusetts has just made a statement during a Congressional session concerning your husband. I'd like to get your comments on it."

"Senator McKinsey?" said Betsy in surprise. "What did he say?"

"That your husband blew up the plane to mask his suicide as an accident."

"WHAT! He must be crazy!" Betsy shouted.

"Well, it IS a fact that the plane was blown up by a bomb, and your husband is the prime suspect," the reporter said.

"I never heard of anything so outrageous! This conversation is over!"

Infuriated, she tried to close the door in the reporter's face. He stood firm and kept trying.

"One more question."

Elise stepped forward and gave the reporter a hard push, saying "Didn't you hear her? Get the hell out of here."

As the door closed the reporter fired his one last question...

"Isn't it true that Mr. Sanders recently took out a million-dollar insurance policy on his life?"

Elise, startled, looked at Betsy who was quivering with rage. She put her arms around Betsy, and hugged her.

"I think you'd better call your lawyer," Elise said.

———

Betsy went to Aaron's office the next morning to discuss this new bombshell. It was difficult for him to get her to address the problem. She kept pacing the room.

"What right has he got to say something like that?" she fumed.

"Betsy, sit down."

"Aaron?"

"Why didn't Neil tell me he had a million-dollar policy?" Aaron asked. "A million dollars, for God's sake!"

"It was five hundred thousand, double indemnity if he died in an accident," said Betsy impatiently.

"You knew about it?" asked Aaron.

"Of course."

"Betsy, what business did Neil have in Miami?"

"How should I know? I don't know anything about his business. That Senator made a terrible accusation, and I don't think he should be allowed to get away with it."

"Why such a large policy?" Aaron pursued.

"I think we should sue him for telling lies about Neil like that. Sue him, Aaron!"

"There's something called 'Congressional immunity'. That means anything that's said on the floor of the Senate is free from suit," explained Aaron.

"Even if it's not true?"

"Even if it's not true. Now please, sit down and answer my question. What reason did Neil have for getting that much insurance?"

Betsy sat down but still could not focus on Aaron's questions. She continued to stew.

"I don't understand that. It's not right."

"Betsy, please. I'm trying to find out if there could possibly be any truth to the statement," Aaron pleaded.

"Truth?" she exploded, "How could there be? Why would Neil want to commit suicide?"

"That's what I'm trying to find out. Were you two having any problems?"

"You mean aside from Renata? No. In fact we were looking forward to our third child."

"Are you telling me you're pregnant?"

"Yes, five or six weeks now."

Aaron felt a pang of guilt over his impatience with her.

"Oh, my," he sighed.

Betsy was not going to let this go.

"Aaron, why would that Senator make a public accusation without any proof?"

"I can only speculate. He's from Massachusetts, and Boston is the headquarters for Nation Air. Maybe they put some pressure on him."

"It's not fair."

"No, it isn't. Betsy, I hate to do this, but I've got to ask you some more questions."

"All right. Go ahead," she said.

"Was he in debt?"

"No."

"Are you sure of that, or are you just guessing?"

"Well...none that I know of anyway. Except the normal things, like the mortgage and car payments."

"Was he in any kind of trouble, or had he been threatened in any way?" Aaron asked.

"He never mentioned anything like that. I don't know why he would be. Everybody liked Neil."

"But why such a large policy?" Aaron asked again.

"You keep asking me that," said Betsy in an agitated manner, "The insurance agent told him that was the amount he should have. Why don't you ask him?"

"They'll have to prove it was a suicide, and since there doesn't seem to be any motive, I don't think you'll have a problem collecting the insurance."

"A good name is to be chosen rather than great riches, and favor is better than silver or gold."

"I beg your pardon?" said Aaron.

"It's from Proverbs. I learned it when I was a little girl."

This signaled to Aaron that the interview was over. He rose, and escorted Betsy to the door. He did have one final matter to cover.

"By the way...I'd rather you didn't discuss this with anyone, even your parents, or read any newspapers, until after the FBI questions you."

"FBI?"

"It's nothing to worry about," he assured her. "Just routine. I'll stall it until I have a chance to look over Neil's records. In the meantime, no newspapers and no news on TV. I mean that."

———

The next day the whole town, in fact the whole country, was buzzing about the mysterious plane crash. Big headlines in the New York Times read:

"LAWYER'S BODY IS DISCOVERED 20 MILES FROM CRASH SITE. INSURANCE PLOT IS HINTED IN PLANE EXPLOSION."

Fred, Joe, Al and Charlie were in their usual seats on the train, the story in the paper their topic of conversation.

"You could get sick reading this," said Joe.

"Why was he twenty miles away?" asked Al.

Charlie leaned over to read Joe's paper and posed a question.

"A million dollars! You didn't think he had any insurance, huh, Fred?"

Fred just shrugged.

"How would it be possible for somebody to bring a bomb aboard an airplane?" asked Joe.

"That's easy," answered Al. "It could be camouflaged as a camera, or a transistor radio."

"Why couldn't the SOB have driven off a cliff, instead of taking all those people with him?" Charlie remarked.

"Hey!" exclaimed Fred. "The guy had his wild side, but he wasn't a psycho. He would never have done this."

"Yeah? So why did he take out a million dollar life insurance policy just two months before? He's guilty as hell, if you ask me."

———

It was time to do something with Neil's clothes and per-sonal belongings. It hurt too much to see his robe on the bathroom door and his shaving equipment in the medicine chest. There was so much to go through. He had an extensive wardrobe. In addition to his business clothes, there were ski outfits, workout clothes. Elise had suggested Betsy donate everything to the Salvation Army. She had also offered to come help sort things out but Betsy wanted to do it alone. It was a way of saying good-bye. There would be some things she wanted to keep, like the black sapphire cuff links and studs he'd worn with his tuxedo the first night they met. He said they were a gift from his father. He kept them in a special case. There was no need to pick out a burial outfit. The coffin had been sealed and she was told she would not be allowed to see him.   They had kept the body a long time at the morgue in New York when it had arrived there. For some reason it had been necessary to do a second autopsy.

Betsy went first to his top dresser drawer where he kept his jewelry case. It wasn't there. It had always been there. Where was it? She looked in every single drawer and it was nowhere to be found. That was peculiar. Maybe Lillian had seen it. She'd have to figure out a way to ask her so that it didn't look as if she was accusing her of taking it. Maybe he had hidden it behind something on the closet shelf. She couldn't quite reach the back so she used a step stool. There was stuff back there that had been there for ages. She smiled when she discovered a clay statue of a Caribbean girl with a fruit basket on her head that she had given Neil as a joke when they were in Venezuela. She took it down and put it on his dresser. It brought back memories of exotic cocktails, and sunny days. She decided to leave it there. It would help her remember the good times.

———

Never would she have thought about going to Venezuela. Neil had come home one evening and shoved a piece of paper under her nose and said, "Here's something for you to sign."

She signed it and then asked, jokingly, "What is it, an excuse from PE?"

"It's an application for a passport."

"You're kidding! Why?"

"It's time we took a real honeymoon."

"The other one wasn't real?"

"The morning sickness put a bit of a damper on it. I want to take you someplace exotic and sexy before you get pregnant again."

"Where are we going? Don't make me guess. If I need a passport that must mean we're going out of the country."

"Brilliant deduction, my dear Watson. We're going to Venezuela."

"Would you say that again so I can be sure I didn't mishear you?"

"I said we're going to Venezuela."

"Why Venezuela?"

"I've never been there, and I've always been intrigued by the name...Venezuela."

"But Neil, we'd have to fly there. You never fly."

"I'm getting a prescription for Miltown. I've heard it chases all your cares away."

It didn't work exactly like that, but somehow Neil survived the flight. Betsy had never been out of the United States except for a photo shoot in Toronto. She was thrilled at her first sight of Caracas from the plane... the mountains rising from the sea...the beautiful turquoise water. They were booked at the Grand Melia, one of Caracas's most luxurious hotels. To Betsy's surprise, a limousine had met them at the airport. Neil was really pulling out all the stops, she thought. She was even more impressed when they arrived at the hotel. The lobby alone resembled a grand ball-room with a white marble staircase leading up to the mezzanine, and potted palms all around. Their suite was equally dramatic. The walls were adorned with original paintings, and the deep set white arm chairs were separated by a polished Queen Anne coffee table. French doors led to a balcony overlooking a lush garden with a pool and a marble fountain. Betsy stepped out onto the balcony and was shocked at shanty towns cascading down the mountainside practically adjacent to the hotel. The contrast to the opulence of the hotel was heart breaking. Neil came up behind her and put his arms around her.

"Don't let that bother you. We won't be leaving the hotel at night."

"That wasn't what I was thinking," said Betsy. They went back into the room. "Are you sure we can afford this?" She went to the door and looked at the rates posted on it. "No, we can't. These rates are obscene! Neil, how are you doing this?"

"It's a once in a lifetime trip, and it's our honeymoon. Why don't you take a relaxing bath while I go down and check on our dinner reservations," Neil suggested.

Betsy had already eyed the enormous marble tub and she felt in need of a bath. She was stretched out in it an hour later with her eyes closed thinking how fortunate they were when Neil came in with a bottle of champagne which he proceeded to pour over her.

"Neil! What are you doing? Are you crazy? You're wasting a bottle of champagne!"

"You deserve every drop. Put a robe on. I've got another bottle on ice. Dinner isn't until ten o'clock."

"Ten o'clock!"

"And that's the early seating. They eat late in this part of the world."

Did they ever get to dinner that night? Betsy couldn't remember.

The following evening Neil took her into the casino. Betsy had never gambled before. Neil showed her how to play roulette. She would only play the red. She won a few dollars on the first play, screamed with excitement, and was ready to quit. Neil laughed and gave her more money to continue, explaining that he would like to go play cards. She was looking at him later across the room at a table with a group of men. They were Hispanic, she noticed. He seemed tense. She hoped he wasn't losing too much.

The next day, Neil had a special treat planned for her. He had booked a massage. The masseuse came to their room with her equipment.

"What about you, Senor? Wouldn't you like a massage, too?" asked the masseuse.

"Neil, it would do you good," said Betsy.

"No, I've got some shopping to do. I'll leave you ladies to it." He kissed Betsy and left. When he returned later he said, "I've got a surprise for you." He threw ten thousand dollars on the bed, all hundreds, saying, "Look what I won playing cards!"

"So that's where you were! In the casino! You said you were going shopping."

"You're not mad, are you?"

"If you'd lost, I'd be mad."

Her father was very skeptical when she told him Neil had won ten thousand playing cards. He had always been a little dubious of Neil for some reason.

"Where did he get the money to get into a game with stakes that high?" he questioned.

———

Betsy spent all afternoon going over Neil's clothes, folding and putting garments in separate piles, holding out a cashmere sweater she wanted for herself and another she thought her father would like, in addition to some ties. Maybe he'd wear one of them to Neil's funeral she mused. She was surprised when Lillian appeared at the door and announced that dinner was ready.

"Oh, my gosh! Where did the time go?" she exclaimed.

Lillian looked around at the piles of clothing. "You certainly have been busy. What are you going to do with all of these?"

"Elise suggested the Salvation Army. Do you have a better idea?" asked Betsy.

"My Church would be very grateful for some of it if that's all right with you."

"Absolutely. Oh, by the way, Lillian, I can't find Neil's little jewelry case. Have you seen it by any chance?"

"Didn't Miss Renata tell you? She came over while you were in the city yesterday, and said she wanted to pick up something that her husband had given Mr. Sanders. She said you knew about it, so I thought it was all right."

"I can't believe her!" exploded Betsy. "Yes, I knew Neil's father had given him the case and the jewelry, but I had no idea she was going to take them. And to do it when I wasn't home! The nerve!"

"I'm sorry, Miss Betsy. I didn't know what to do."

"It's not your fault, Lillian. She's the one who was wrong. I'll be down in a minute."

She had really wanted to keep those studs and cuff links. If Renata had asked, Betsy thought to herself, she probably would have given them to her. But this was a major invasion of privacy. She had no right to do that! What else was she capable of? Betsy had a bad feeling this would not be the last time Renata would impose her will.

SEVEN

A funeral was planned for Neil Sanders at the Jewish Cemetery as per his mother's wishes. However, some misleading statements by Reverend Bill Brooks led the press to believe it was going to be held at the Lutheran Church, in order to keep them from intruding on the family's grief. The Jewish cemetery, normally lush with greenery and shade trees, was covered with snow and the trees were bare.

The family and guests were gathered in the cold, dreary foyer, waiting for the hearse to arrive. Francine and Jerry were among the group, and for once Francine refrained from using foul language. No one noticed a small, black Mercedes with 1960 Florida license plates stop at the gate. The car stood for a few moments, engine idling, then drove away. The hearse arrived shortly after. Workers opened the door and removed the casket. Mr. Johnson was heard to remark, "Well, the body has arrived, and Renata isn't here yet. She's going to make her usual grand entrance. Even at her son's funeral."

And, that is exactly what she did. She was dressed in an elegant black suit, veiled hat, and a mink coat with a diamond broach. Her silver hair was beautifully coiffed. She was helped out of her limousine by the chauffeur and, escorted by her friends, the Lewins, she made her way through the crusted snow toward the foyer. Betsy went out to meet her and they shared a stiff embrace.

Back in the foyer Fred and Elise Rosen had a strange conversation. Elise suddenly, out of the blue, said, "I'm going to introduce Betsy to Arthur Anderson."

"Elise!" Fred was shocked beyond belief.

"I don't know what made me say that! I didn't even know I was thinking it. It just came out."

"Well, I certainly hope no one else heard it."

When everyone had assembled, the mourners began the solemn trek to the gravesite, led by Rabbi Goldstein. Before they started he had pinned a black cloth ribbon on the left shoulders of Betsy and Renata. The coffin was carried by Fred Rosen, Mr. Lewin, Aaron Ross, Betsy's father, and two colleagues of Neil's that Betsy barely knew. Betsy and her mother, Katie, walked directly behind the coffin, with their arms around each other. Renata followed, arm in arm with Mrs. Lewin. All others brought up the rear.

Betsy was fighting tears. She whispered to her mother, "I just can't believe Neil is in there. For the first time, I understand an open coffin."

"I don't know. I have mixed feelings about it," said Katie.

Suddenly she noticed Betsy's hand on her stomach and her pained expression.

"What is it?'

"Oh, Mother...it feels like I'm getting my period, but I can't be."

At the gravesite, everyone remained standing except Betsy and Renata, who were seated facing the grave. Aaron gave a short eulogy, extolling Neil's virtues as a husband and father and his generosity to various charities. After the coffin was lowered, the Rabbi stood in front of Betsy and Renata, leaned forward, and taking a small penknife, he made a cut in the black ribbons pinned on their shoulders and ripped the cloth. Betsy had never experienced anything like this. She was startled, but found it strangely moving. The Rabbi then said a prayer:

"Baruch at adonai elohainu melech ha-olam dayan ha-emet. Blessed are Thou, Lord our God, the true Judge."

The Rabbi held out a shovel to Betsy. She looked at him in confusion. The Rabbi explained: "You are to throw the first shovelful of dirt...to bury him."

Betsy didn't move. She was frozen. Renata reached out aggressively and grabbed the shovel. The Rabbi gently disengaged her hand. He shook his head and in a kind voice, said, "No. The wife is first."

He extended the shovel to Betsy again, and took her hand to help her stand up. She took the shovel, and tried to dig into the frozen mound of earth. Finally she got a clod of dirt on the blade of the shovel and tossed it onto the coffin. It landed with a loud thud. Betsy fainted and fell into the snow beside the open grave.

———

Dr. Katz, a balding man in his late 60's, wearing glasses, was seated beside Betsy on her bed. After having examined her, he gave her reassurance.

"Nothing to worry about."

"Nothing to worry about? Did you see that horde of reporters in my front yard?"

"Don't concern yourself with them. You have to take care of yourself and the baby right now. My advice is that you stay off your feet completely for a few days."

"I'm not going to the hospital!"

"You can stay home if you promise to stay in bed."

"They made awful accusations about Neil," Betsy lamented, "and they keep hounding me with questions. It's scaring the children, too. They can't even go out to play in the backyard without some reporter taking a picture of them over the fence."

"That's terrible. Children shouldn't have to put up with things like that," said the doctor, sympathetically.

"That's not the worst of it. Sven won't go to his preschool because some of the kids won't play with him. They say his daddy did something bad. I know it's coming from lies they've printed in the paper."

"They're too young to read," Dr Katz said with a shake of his head. "The parents are at fault. They should be ashamed of themselves."

"Please don't tell them I'm pregnant or they'll never leave me alone," begged Betsy.

"I promise they won't get any information out of me," he said. "You stay in bed now. That's an order! I'll come back to see you tomorrow."

"Thank you so much for coming, Dr. Katz," said Betsy, gratefully. "I know you're officially retired, but I didn't know who else to call."

"This is a special circumstance. I'm glad you called."

A few moments after Dr. Katz left, Betsy disobeyed orders and got out of bed. She went to the window and peeked through the blind. What she saw were four reporters surrounding the doctor. The brash, young reporter from 'The Town Crier' was right in his face. She could not hear what they were saying, but she saw the doctor shaking his head and holding his hand up, obviously signaling 'no comment.' They pursued him all the way to his car.

Katie Johnson entered the room and saw Betsy standing at the window. She said to her sternly, "Get back in bed! You heard what the doctor said."

Betsy reluctantly obeyed, saying to her mother, "When is this nightmare going to end?"

———

Aaron was in the mood for a relaxing lunch at his club. He was a member of the Yale Club of New York, located on Vanderbilt and 44th Street in Manhattan, membership restricted to alumni and faculty of Yale University, the largest private club in the world. It's neighbors include the Harvard Club, the N.Y. Yacht Club and the Bar Association of New York. Aaron chose to lunch in the Lounge, a large room with a high, ornate ceiling and wood paneled walls, lined with fireplaces and distinguished portraits of past Presidents. He was seated at a table by the window reading the New York Times, the headlines of which read:

"SANDERS WIDOW CLAIMS ILLNESS. UNCONFIRMED BY DOCTOR."

A short, stocky, stylishly dressed man, scotch and soda in hand, slipped into the chair opposite Aaron. This was Hank Beatty, attorney with Eastern Mutual Insurance Company.

"Aaron, mind if I join you?" he asked, but did not wait for an answer before seating himself. "I understand you're representing the Sanders widow."

"You're remarkably well informed, Beatty," said Aaron.

"I usually am," Beatty replied arrogantly.

"So, what kind of game are we playing today?"

Beatty spread his arms and smiled ingratiatingly. "Hey, c'mon. I'm here to make things easier for you."

"In what way?" Aaron asked.

"You know we don't pay off on suicides."

"It wasn't a suicide," Aaron said indignantly.

"I'm trying to do you a favor here, and you refuse an offer before it's even made."

"I'm not interested in any offers. A five hundred-thousand dollar policy with double indemnity entitles my client to one million dollars, not a penny less."

Beatty raised his drink in salute. "Well...here's mud in your eye."

"That's appropriate," Aaron remarked.

Beatty laughed, not bothered at all. "Has the FBI interrogated her yet?"

"No, she's been ill."

"So I've read. I predict you'll want to continue this conversation after they're done with her."

"Is that a threat?"

"Only if you feel threatened."

Beatty rose, taking his drink with him. Watching him depart, Aaron had a worried look on his face, wondering if there was something Beatty knew that he didn't.

———

Renata paid a visit to Betsy while she was still in bed under doctor's orders. She sat in a chair beside the bed while the two children played with toys on the floor. She was on a campaign to get Betsy to allow the children to visit her in Florida. Pitching in a relentless manner, she said, "I can't understand what your objection is. I have a beautiful condominium right on the beach, and full time help. It would be the best thing in the world for them... the poor little orphans."

"Don't call them that!" Betsy scolded her. "They're not orphans."

The conversation distracted Sven from his toy. He looked up and asked, "What's an orphan?"

Betsy threw Renata an angry look, which was ignored.

"An orphan is someone whose mother and father have both died," Betsy explained. "You are not an orphan."

Renata carried on as if that conversation had never occurred. "Give me one good reason why you don't want them to go."

"They need to be with their mother. At this time, more than ever," said Betsy.

"But what good are you doing them up here in bed?"

"It's not terminal, you know."

Ana climbed up on Renata's knees, "Do horsey, Grandma, do horsey."

At first Renata ignored her, still trying to convince Betsy.

"I don't know why you're being so stubborn," she pressed on.

Ana again implored, "Do horsey, Grandma!"

Renata gave in, and holding Ana's hands, began to give her a horsey ride. She accompanied this in a sing-song voice:

"This is the way the lady rides, the lady rides, the lady rides. This is the way the lady rides, so early in the morning." Then she stopped.

Ana wanted more. "Do cowboy! Do cowboy!"

Renata got a sad look on her face and said, "If only your daddy were here. Nobody can do cowboy as good as he." Ana started to cry.

Betsy was furious. "Stop doing that, Renata!"

Sven spoke up again. "Daddy wouldn't have died if we'd been there to take him to the hospital."

"That's not so, Sven," Betsy explained, "there was nothing anyone could do. He died before he reached the ground."

"You don't have to give him such a graphic description," said Renata.

"I want to make sure he understands that nothing could have been done. For some reason, he feels guilty."

"You see?" Renata pounced. "He needs to get away from this place."

"This 'place' is their home."

Thankfully, they were interrupted by Lillian's appearance in the doorway.

"Mr. Ross is here. Is it all right for him to come up?"

"By all means," said Betsy. Then to Renata when Lillian had left the room, "I'd like to talk with Aaron privately, if you don't mind."

Renata drew herself up regally. "Why should I mind? Come, children, we'll get out of your mother's way."

She picked up a couple of toys from the floor and was herding the children out of the room when she encountered Aaron. She greeted him with a kiss on the cheek "Aaron, darling, how nice to see you." And, as a parting remark, "Perhaps you can talk some sense into Betty."

"It's BETSY!" came a howl from the bed.

Aaron sat in the chair vacated by Renata and asked Betsy, "What was that all about?"

"She wants to take the children to Florida for two weeks."

"That sounds like a great idea."

"She plays on their emotions. I don't think she's healthy for them."

"Aren't you blowing it out of proportion?" asked Aaron. "What harm could she do to them in a couple of weeks?"

"You'd be surprised."

"A little rest wouldn't hurt you a bit either. Let them go," he urged.

"I'll think about it."

"How are you feeling?"

"At the end of my rope…is that why you came? Just to ask how I'm feeling?"

"The FBI is getting antsy about talking to you, and I can't keep stalling them. They don't believe you're sick, and if you don't cooperate soon, it'll look as if you're trying to hide something."

"What could there possibly be to hide?" she asked.

"I don't want any surprises," Aaron said.

"What kind of surprises?"

"If there are any secrets at all, now is the time to tell me."

"Aaron, there are no secrets. We were just an ordinary married couple. Neil was a wonderful husband and father."

"And you loved each other?"

"Very much. You know that."

"Then, I guess we don't have anything to worry about. I'll arrange for them to question you in my office. It'll be more comfortable for you."

After Aaron left, Betsy thought about what he had said about Renata taking the children to Florida. Maybe she should let them go...get them away from the reporters. Perhaps it would help their relationship, too. Renata had been a thorn in her side throughout the marriage. She shuddered remembering how unpleasant their first meeting had been.

EIGHT

In Aaron's modest Law Office on East 45th Street in Manhattan, John O'Brien of the FBI and his associate, Harry Carter, were waiting to interrogate Betsy. John, a tall, handsome, sandy haired Irishman, in his mid-30's, was an ex-Navy pilot. He was the type who'd seen it all. Thoroughly professional. Harry was African-American, in his late 30's. He possessed an innate sense of humor that was difficult to suppress. His job was to do the taping.

Aaron's secretary, Julie, popped her head in to announce that Betsy had arrived. Aaron stood up to greet Betsy when she came through the door. John swung around in his chair in a blasé manner. He was surprised. She wasn't what he expected at all. This was a lady, not some ditzy babe. As an afterthought, he also stood. Betsy extended her hand to each of the men as Aaron introduced them.

"I realize this is not pleasant for you, Mrs. Sanders. I'll try to make it as easy as possible," began John.

She was advised they would be taping the interview. After she sat down, Harry turned on the recorder and John continued, "May I call you Betsy?"

Betsy nodded her assent. Clearly, she was quite tense.

"Let's see, You are twenty-seven years old, right?'

"Yes."

"Where were you born?"

"Topeka, Kansas."

"Did you go to college?"

"Yes, I went to Knox, in Galesburg."

"Graduate?

"Yes, class of '53.

"That's a pricey school. Were you on a scholarship?"

"Partial. I paid the rest myself by working in the summer."

"Good for you. What kind of work did you do, Betsy?"

"I was a corn de-tasseler."

They all did a double take, including Aaron.

"Say what?" Harry chuckled.

"Would you explain that?" asked John.

"The male seed corn tassels are used to pollinate the female corn. The pollen producing flowers, or the tassels, are removed from the tops of the corn in every other row. They become female plants. The male plants, the ones which are not de-tasseled, then pollinate the silk on the de-tasseled female corn. They have machines to remove the tassels now, but it used to be done by hand. That's what I did."

They stared at her in amazement. Then Harry started to laugh out loud. John tried not to, but he couldn't control the smile spreading on his face. It was contagious. Aaron started to laugh, too. Then the humor of it hit Betsy and she joined in. When the laughter finally stopped, Betsy was much more relaxed. Her normal, bubbly personality started to emerge.

John had to restore order. He continued with the interview.

"Did you come to New York to model?"

"No, I had hoped to be a designer. I started modeling to support myself so I could go to design school."

"What school did you attend?"

"I didn't go. Things changed when I met Neil at a party. We were married within three months."

"Were you married in New York?"

"The first time. We were married here by a Judge and then two months later we were married by a minister in my home town Church. We hadn't told my parents we'd been married, and when Sven was born early I had a time explaining it then."

"I guess they were happy to be grandparents though."

"Yes, they were. That's why they moved to Connecticut."

"Would you say you had a happy marriage?"

"Yes, very. It was everything I ever dreamed of."

John paused a moment. Then...

"I'm a little confused. You paint a picture of a happy couple, yet you went for marriage counseling in the second year. Why?"

Betsy looked over at Aaron. She was surprised they knew this. Aaron gestured that she should answer.

"His mother interfered a lot. In her eyes no woman was good enough for her son, especially a farmer's daughter. She used to call Neil all the time and run me down. He finally quit taking most of her calls. He'd have me say he was out."

"Did it bother you to lie to his mother for him?"

"Yes, as a matter of fact, it did. I always felt he should have stood up to her more."

"Were you involved at all with your husband's business dealings?"

"No. I wasn't. He never wanted me to come to his office because he said some of his clients were unsavory characters and he didn't want me to have any contact with them."

"Did you file a joint income tax?"

"Yes."

"Ever read it?"

"No. He'd just put something in front of me and say 'sign it' and I would."

"Did he do this with other documents as well?"

Betsy thought a moment before answering.

"Yes. A few times."

"But you had complete trust in him?"

"Of course. If a wife can't trust her own husband, who's she going to trust?"

"Exactly," said John, a bit cynically Betsy thought.

He rifled through some papers in a folder and addressed her again.

"Did he go out of town a lot?"

"He took a trip about once a month."

"Didn't you ever go with him?"

"No. They were usually very short...just a couple of days."

"How did you spend your evenings when he was gone?"

"I'd catch up on my sewing."

"Sewing," said John as if he didn't believe her.

"Yes. I like to sew. I never could get much done when Neil was home."

"Weren't you lonesome when he was away?"

"Of course. But I never played around, if that's what you're insinuating."

Harry coughed, enjoying the rebuff. John glanced over disapprovingly. He was on a mission.

"I've heard that your husband didn't care for flying. Why did he fly that fateful night?"

"Time, I guess. I wanted him to take the train...especially when it started to snow, but he said he had an early morning appointment."

"Were you with him right up until the plane left, Betsy?"

"No. It was snowing, and he thought I should go on home. He called later to make sure I got there okay."

"What time was that?"

"It was a little after ten I think, maybe even ten thirty. I was already in bed. He told me the flight was delayed again, and wouldn't take off until after midnight. They had divided it into two flights because there wasn't another large plane available. He was nervous about flying in a smaller plane, so I suggested again that he take the midnight train. He could have still made it. He said he might. When the airline called me in the morning to tell me about the crash, I thought it was Neil calling to say he hadn't been on that plane."

"Wait a minute. You knew about the crash before the airline called?"

"I'd heard it on the radio. But even before that, the person who was supposed to meet Neil in Miami called early in the morning, and told me the plane was missing."

John leaned forward, raising an eyebrow in disbelief.

"Oh, really? What is the name of this person?"

"I don't remember."

"I can't believe you don't remember something that important," John commented.

"I was half asleep" Betsy protested. "The phone had awakened me, and it woke the baby up, too. She was crying...then he hung up on me..."

"He hung up on you? He paused. "Mrs. Sanders..."

Betsy looked up with a slight frown. There was a change in the tone of his voice and his attitude. He had called her Mrs. Sanders instead of Betsy.

John continued..."Did you know about the insurance your husband purchased recently?"

"Of course," answered Betsy.

"Was it your idea for him to take out this policy?"

"No, Neil made all those kinds of decisions."

"What prompted him to take out such a large amount?"

"I'm so tired of that question," said Betsy impatiently. "Why don't you ask the insurance salesman? He's the one who told Neil how much he needed."

John made a note of that.

"I'll do that," he said, then added, "When you collect this sizable amount of insurance you'll be able to do anything you want, won't you? What are your plans?"

"I haven't given that any thought."

"That's hard to believe. You obviously like nice clothes," he said, eyeing the Chanel suit she was wearing. "Then there's your career in designing that was interrupted by marriage."

"I have no regrets. My life has been very fulfilling... up until now."

"Still" John pressed on, "a million dollars is a lot of money." He paused. "People have killed for a lot less than that."

Betsy was furious. Her eyes were flashing as she responded.

"I thought you were asking funny questions. You're accusing me!"

"No, no, we're not accusing you of anything. You must admit however, that you certainly had a motive."

"What motive? Money can't make up for the loss of a husband, and a father for my children."

"Does the name 'Sky Blue' mean anything to you?"

Betsy was perplexed, wondering where that had come from.

"I've heard her name, who could forget it? I think she's a model, but I don't know her. Why on earth would you ask me that?"

John did not answer at first. He appeared to be weighing something in his mind. When he did speak, he looked piercingly into Betsy's eyes in order to measure her response.

"We've had your husband under surveillance for some time, and we know for a fact that Sky Blue was his mistress. She accompanied him on many of his so called business trips. So, it's not necessary for you to protect him."

Betsy was stunned. This was the last thing in the world she expected. She was hit by the same shock waves as when she heard about Neil's death. Her pain was so obvious, and so naked that the men were embarrassed to be witnessing it. They exchanged glances, and Harry stopped the recorder.

"I think this about wraps it up, wouldn't you say, John?" Harry asked.

"Sure, Harry. For now anyway. Thank you, Mrs. Sanders."

Betsy did not respond. She had withdrawn into her own private Hell. Harry gathered up the tape recorder, and Aaron walked the two men to the door. As they were leaving John spoke to Aaron in a low voice.

"Don't forget to advise her she's not to leave the State."

"She lives in Connecticut, John."

"I realize that. Of course she can go home, but you know what I mean."

Aaron nodded and closed the door. He pulled a chair close in front of Betsy and took her hands in his.

"My God, Betsy, I'm sorry. If there was any way to avoid it…"

Betsy pulled her hands away from him and looked at him accusingly.

"But you knew it! Why didn't you tell me? At least give me some warning."

"I was counting on the fact that you didn't know. It's terribly important they believe you're telling the truth… about everything."

"What did he mean they had Neil under surveillance? What for?"

"Betsy, I can't..."

"I want an answer!"

"I can't tell you. Right now the best thing we've got going is your faith in Neil. I don't want that to be destroyed."

"But it's all right to tell me he had a girlfriend...which I don't believe by the way. What other stories are they coming up with? I need to know."

"Betsy, if you start digging, you're going to blow the whole thing. This case depends on your credibility, and I want you to be telling the truth when they ask you if you know about certain things. If you think this was ugly, wait until the insurance company's lawyers start in on you. They don't want to pay."

"Forget about the insurance then. I don't care about the money."

"Are you crazy!...I'm sorry. I shouldn't have said that...now listen to me carefully. You have no income... zero. I've been going through Neil's files, and some of those things Neil had you sign were loans for which you are now responsible. You are deeply in debt. You could lose everything. Your house, your kid's education... everything. You desperately need that insurance."

Betsy was stunned. Aaron continued in a kinder tone:

"Besides...if you don't file the claim, it'll look like you believe it was suicide. You don't believe that, do you?"

"No! I'll never believe that!"

"But everyone else will, unless you file the claim. And, incidentally, you'll be lucky if you end up with a quarter of it after everything's been paid off."

"And my remaining ignorant is going to make a difference?"

"Not ignorant...innocent."

She got up to leave and, as Aaron was walking her to the door, he again instructed her to not read any newspapers or discuss the case with anyone.

"I just want his name to be cleared," Betsy said.

"We'll have a better chance of doing that if you listen to me. Oh, one more thing...I was asked to tell you you're not allowed to leave the State."

Betsy left without answering.

—

John and Harry sat in the coffee shop across the street from Aaron's office at a table by the window that had a good view of the entrance to Aaron's office building. They were discussing the interview.

"What do you think?" Harry asked.

"She seems so vulnerable, but it could be a performance."

"Anything is possible. Hey...she just came out..."

John rose from the table quickly.

"I'm going to follow her," he said. "Tell Paul I'll check in tonight with my report."

John began to follow Betsy and neither he nor she noticed the black Mercedes, slowly following also.

Betsy stopped at the first phone booth she came to. She entered and opened the phone book, which was attached by a chain. Her finger went down the list of names, stopping at S. Blue. She took a dime from her purse and dropped it into the slot. She started to dial, but couldn't finish. She leaned on the phone and started to cry.

Suddenly, she seemed to go crazy. Holding her purse by the strap, she began to beat on the telephone. She landed blow after blow, all the while screaming:

"I loved you! I trusted you! You liar! Liar! You bastard!"

Her energy spent, she left the booth, looking as if she had lost everything in the world.

John stopped following, and regarded her with sympathy. For a moment he was tempted to go after her. The temptation passed, and he turned around to go back to the coffee shop. It was then that he became aware of the black Mercedes. Some instinct caused him to note the Florida license plates.

NINE

That night, when Betsy entered her bedroom and turned on the lamp, the light fell on a framed wedding picture of herself and Neil. Still burning with anger, she slammed the picture face downward on the night table, breaking the glass in the frame. Directly following, there was another sound of breaking glass. It came from downstairs in the living room. Alarmed, Betsy ran down the stairs to see what had caused it and found that a large rock had been thrown through the window. There was a note tied to it with string. Frightened, but curious, she took it off. The note was printed in crayon. It read:

"Wife of a murderer. You should die too."

She immediately ran to the kitchen phone to call Aaron. He commented that he'd been afraid there were going to be a few kooks around, and that was why he thought it was a good idea for Renata to take the children to Florida.

"What if they break in?" asked Betsy, nearing hysteria.

"Don't worry," said Aaron, "Whoever did that is probably miles away by now, but I'm going to call the police and ask for protection."

"Should I...Ohhh" She doubled over in pain.

""What's the matter? Are you all right?" he asked.

"Just a cramp. Darn! I thought that had stopped." Betsy groaned.

"Maybe you should call the doctor." he suggested.

"No, it's gone now. Probably just indigestion," she said.

"Could be stress. Try and stay calm now. I'm going to call the Police and the FBI, too."

Betsy went back in the living room and cleaned up the broken glass. There was a cold draft coming in the window so she found some duct tape in a kitchen drawer and looked for something to tape over the window. If only she hadn't stopped the newspaper, she thought, she could have used that. She finally settled on a grocery bag, and sealed the window as best she could. She'd call someone tomorrow to fix it, she told herself. She then went back upstairs and picked up the glass from the night table and set the picture back up again, ashamed she'd let her temper get the best of her.

The phone was ringing when Betsy stepped out of the shower later. Still dripping, she wrapped a towel around herself, went into the bedroom and answered it.

The person on the other end of the phone identi- fied himself as special agent, O'Brien, FBI. He was in an automobile parked where he had a clear view of the Sanders' house.

"What is it now?" asked Betsy.

"It was just a couple of teenagers who threw the rock. The Police have them now. I'll see that it doesn't happen again," said John.

"And how do you propose to do that pray tell?"

"There'll be somebody here."

Betsy turned off the lamp, and still holding the phone to her ear, went to the window and looked out. She saw him in the car. He was all bundled up against the cold, wearing a woolen scarf and hat. She felt a little bit sorry for him. A little bit.

"Oh, the fox is guarding the hen house."

John grinned. "You can go to sleep now."

Betsy hung up the phone, wrapped the towel around her tighter, and then went back to peek out the window again.

———

There were headlines about the crash every day. That day's were:

"CHARGES OF EMBEZZLEMENT AND FRAUD LEVELED AT DECEASED ATTORNEY."

Aboard the commuter train Joe was reading the Times as Charlie was dealing. Al and Fred picked up their cards.

"Anything new?" Charlie asked.

"Yeah, Marilyn Monroe married Joe DiMaggio," Joe said.

"That's not new. I meant about Sanders. Isn't that what you're reading about?"

"Yeah," Joe said, "he was collecting funds for some hospital but the hospital never got 'em."

"What does his wife have to say about all this stuff they've uncovered, Fred?" Charlie wanted to know.

"You'll find this hard to believe," said Fred, "but she doesn't even know about it. Elise says she won't read a newspaper or watch television, or even talk about him."

"It's incredible," said Joe, still reading. "The D.A., the FBI and the Bar Association were all after him."

"It sure gives him a motive for suicide" remarked Charlie, "He was heading for a wipeout."

"You didn't know this guy," Fred answered. "He had enough chutzpah to think he could beat any rap. He'd never kill himself."

"If his wife can convince the insurance company of that, she's going to be one rich broad." He scooped up the cards and winked. "Say hello to the merry widow for me."

TEN

It was while she was shopping in the grocery store that Betsy noticed people were avoiding her as if she had the plague. Some pretended they didn't see her, but one woman actually turned her cart around to go in the opposite direction when they were about to meet in the aisle. The exception was the butcher, Gordon, a brawny, red-headed chap.

"Good afternoon, Mrs. Sanders, what can I do for you today?" Gordon asked pleasantly.

"That rump roast looks good. I haven't had any of that for a while," she answered.

He reached into the counter to retrieve the roast, all the while keeping his eyes on her. As he wrapped the roast in brown butcher's paper, he said, "I haven't had any good rump for a while myself."

She heard a nearby customer snicker. He couldn't possibly have meant what that sounded like, she thought. Or, could he?

Then he said, "I'd be happy to deliver meat to you at home any time." And, he winked in a lascivious manner when he handed her the package.

Betsy, mortified, decided to ignore it. She finished shopping, trying not to listen to the whispers, or pay notice to the side-long glances at the check-out counter. It was while carrying her bag of groceries out of the store that she saw it.

There was a news stand smack in her line of vision. Big headlines read:

"SANDERS SUSPECTED OF HANDLING FUNDS FOR GAMBLING SYNDICATE AND OTHER RACKETEERS"

———

This was the first time since Neil died that she had seen a newspaper. She had dutifully followed Aarons instructions to avoid doing so. She was shocked and revolted by what she had seen, and rushed home to phone Aaron.

"How am I supposed to forget something that I saw," she screamed at him, "I can't un-see it. I don't understand what's going on."

Aaron was in a tough spot. She was already very upset and he had more bad news to give her. There was no way to prepare her or soften the blow, so he gave it to her straight.

"Renata has instituted proceedings in Florida to gain custody of the children." Before she could say anything, he added, "There's no way she can get away with it though."

Betsy was so stunned she could not speak for a moment. She clutched her stomach and cried out, "NOT my children!"

She would not even listen to Aaron's apologies for having talked her into letting Renata take the children. She could only hysterically repeat, "We have to get them back! We have to get them back!"

"We will get them back. I promise you," Aaron assured her.

"How?? Tell me how!" She was crying. "She's an evil person! How could she do this?"

"Get to my office as early as you can tomorrow and we'll discuss the best way to handle the situation."

"Situation? She's kidnapped my children, and you call it a SITUATION!"

"Betsy, I can't do anything right now. Don't worry, I'll take care of it tomorrow."

"Don't WORRY?"

There was no response. He had hung up.

Betsy immediately dialed her parents' home and requested they both come over right away. She said it was urgent and she didn't want to talk about it on the phone.

A short time later, an FBI agent, who was staked out down the street, watching the Sanders house, made an entry in his notebook as to what time the Johnsons arrived.

Inside, Betsy had been busy. She had packed a large satchel purse with a pair of nylon-tricot pajamas, a change of underwear, some cosmetics and a toothbrush. After the Johnsons had been there for about an hour, the agent made a note in his notebook as to the time they left. What he didn't know is that it was Betsy, wearing her mother's coat, and a scarf over her head, who left with Mr. Johnson.

ELEVEN

The train was in motion, swaying and vibrating in time to the clickity-clack of the wheels, punctuated occasionally by a mournful whistle when it came to a crossing.

Betsy was asleep in her berth. It was a fitful sleep, tossing and turning, moaning from time to time. Something awakened her. She felt as if she was being smothered and with a guttural cry, threw the covers off and turned on the light. She looked down in horror at the blood spreading darkly over the berth. She reached up to ring the bell for the porter and then fainted.

When she regained consciousness a doctor was bending over her wiping her face with a wet towel. It was 4:00 A.M. in the morning. The train had stopped in a small town in South Carolina. The doctor had boarded the train there and was led to Betsy's compartment by the porter. He introduced himself and started to question her.

"I'm Dr. Moore. Can you tell me what happened?" he asked.

"I don't know..."

"Are you in any pain?" he asked.

"No. Something woke me up, and there was all this blood."

"Did you know that you were pregnant?"

"Yes, I am. Oh my God! Oh, no! I've lost the baby, haven't I?"

"I'm afraid so," he said sympathetically. "We're going to take you off the train and put you in a hospital."

Betsy started to cry. "I have to get to Miami. I can't get off the train."

"You don't have a choice," said the doctor, "you've lost a great deal of blood."

Betsy was taken to a small hospital, given a tiny, barren, private room, and hooked up to an I.V. which delivered saline and glucose to her, a drop at a time. She couldn't have been more miserable.

When Aaron showed up in the afternoon, she cried with relief.

"Aaron, thank God! Get me out of here as quick as you can!"

"Hey, not so fast," he responded. "How are you feeling?"

"I've got to get there before she knows I'm coming," she said, hysterically.

"Betsy, calm down. You're going to pull that thing out of your arm."

"I want my children!"

"Will you listen to me?"

"I never should have listened to you!" she said accusingly.

"As soon as I walk out of here, I'm going to Miami to get them. Today!" Aaron promised.

"I knew I couldn't trust her! I'm going with you. Get me OUT of here!" Betsy implored.

"I can't do that. You're in no condition. Besides, you were ordered not to leave the State."

"She's trying to take my children away from me! Don't you understand?"

"I do understand, but the FBI doesn't."

"I don't care about the FBI..."

Aaron interrupted, "There's an agent out in the hall who will be bringing you home as soon as the doctor releases you."

"When will that be?"

"If you follow the doctor's orders..."

He stopped as Dr. Moore entered the room.

"How's my patient doing?" the doctor asked.

"I'm hoping you can tell me," Aaron said. "How long do you think it'll be before she can leave?"

"She'll be all right by tomorrow, if she'll rest," he replied.

"Stop talking about me as if I weren't here," Betsy protested.

Aaron leaned over and kissed her on the forehead.

"I'm leaving," he said. "You behave now."

"Do you swear you're going to get the children? That's all I care about."

"I'm on my way. Take good care of her, Doc."

"You can count on that," Dr. Moore assured him.

The doctor followed Aaron out of the room in order to speak to him privately. FBI agent, John O'Brien, was sitting in a chair in the hall.

"Mr. Ross..." Dr. Moore began.

"Yes?"

"There have been quite a few reporters asking to talk to Mrs. Sanders. I really don't think she should be disturbed."

"I couldn't agree with you more." He turned to the agent. "John, will you make sure no reporters get to her?"

"Nobody goes in...nobody goes out," promised John.

———

Long after midnight a nurse came with a container of coffee for John, who was still sitting in the corridor. He accepted it gratefully.

"It might be kinda strong," the nurse said.

"Perfect," replied John, "thank you."

The hospital lights had been lowered and there was a hushed atmosphere. Sipping his coffee, John got up and walked to the half open door of Betsy's room. He saw she was asleep. She looks like an alabaster angel, he thought. Struck by her fragile beauty, he gazed at her for a long time.

———

The following day, John and Betsy were seated facing each other in a private compartment on the train taking them north. Both were looking out the window. John was surprised when Betsy suddenly started to giggle.

"What's so funny?" he asked.

"You'll probably think I'm weird or something, but it just seems so silly. Me...a murder suspect...and you...sitting here guarding me. I was thinking of all those movies I've seen where the lawman is taking the outlaw back, and he always handcuffs himself to him on the train."

John grinned. "I happen to have some handcuffs, and I'll be glad to oblige."

"No, thanks."

Their eyes met. Betsy looked away, embarrassed. This was the first nonprofessional exchange they had shared. She suddenly realized he was a very appealing man, and felt guilty, and disloyal to Neil, for even thinking it. She sneaked another look at him, and caught him sneaking one at her, too. She decided to take advantage of the changed atmosphere. She spoke in a half kidding, half serious manner.

"Do you really think I killed my husband?"

"I always believe a person is innocent until they're proven guilty," he answered.

"Then you must believe Neil is innocent, too."

"I'm sorry, but I can't discuss that with you," he said.

"I should have expected that," Betsy said disgustedly. "For a minute there, I thought you were human."

John's eyes bore into her.

"I'm human."

Betsy looked away again, all sorts of emotions stirring within her. She decided to try again.

"Can I ask you just one question?" she ventured.

"I can't promise you an answer," he said.

"Do you really know for a fact that Sky Blue was my husband's girlfriend?"

"I'm afraid so."

"Have you ever met her personally?"

"You said one question."

Their eyes met again, and he grinned, guessing what it was she wanted to know.

"She's not nearly as pretty as you."

Betsy smiled in spite of herself. She was embarrassed, but still flattered. They sat a few moments in silence and Betsy spoke again, more to herself than to John.

"Finding out he had a girlfriend was almost as bad as his dying. How could I have missed the signs? There must have been some signs. I thought I knew him so well. I can't understand why he would do that. He said he loved me...and I always tried to be a good wife."

"Some people don't feel free unless they're running from something," said John.

"Were you a philosopher before you joined the FBI?" asked Betsy in a kidding tone.

"No, I was in the Navy. But then I guess you have to be pretty philosophical to make it in the Navy," he answered.

Betsy laughed appreciatively. They continued a friendly conversation during lunch in the dining car. John was telling Betsy about an incident he had in the Navy.

"We were on leave in Japan. I got roaring drunk. The last thing I remember was two Army guys jumping me in the alley. I had two hundred dollars on me, so I fought like crazy. The next morning, I woke up on the ship and I had FOUR hundred dollars in my pocket, and couldn't remember a thing! That's the last time I ever got drunk."

"That's a funny story," Betsy commented.

After a few minutes, she asked, "Are you married?"

"Was. I had just gotten a 'Dear John' letter that day. That's why I got drunk."

"That explains it!" she announced.

"Explains what?"

"Why you immediately jumped to the conclusion that I wasn't alone the nights Neil was away."

"Hmmm. How would you like a job with the FBI?"

TWELVE

John and Betsy were pushing through the crowd in Penn Station, John running interference for her, when they were abruptly halted by two men blocking their way One of the men asked Betsy if she was Betsy Sanders. John answered for her:

"What is it you want?" he asked.

"I have something for Betsy Sanders. Is that you?" he replied while holding out an envelope toward her.

"Yes, what is it?" Betsy asked as she took the envelope.

"It's a summons!" John said.

The two men disappeared into the crowd.

Betsy opened the envelope, took out the summons and began to read it. She turned to John, shocked.

"They're suing me! The insurance company is suing ME! But how can they sue me? What for?"

John took a look at the summons.

"They say you've filed a fraudulent claim."

"What does that mean?"

"It means they're trying to put the burden of proof on you to prove Neil didn't commit suicide, instead of their having to prove he did. You'll have to file a countersuit. You'd better call your lawyer as soon as possible."

———

The minute Aaron got back from retrieving the children, Betsy went straight to his office. She paced back and forth in the office, extremely agitated.

"I want you to investigate every passenger on that plane," she stated.

"I can't do that," said Aaron, "it would cost a fortune."

"How much?" Betsy asked.

"Thousands!"

A Good Name

"Maybe I can borrow the money."

"Betsy, be sensible. You're already deeply in debt... more than you can imagine. If you're willing to compromise, I think I can make a deal."

"What kind of deal? You want me to say I think he's guilty?"

"No, I didn't say that."

"If I settle, that's what I'd be saying, isn't it?" Betsy countered. "Remember, that's why you said I had to file the claim."

"Betsy..."

She sat down to face Aaron,.

"It's not the money, Aaron." Her voice began to break, "Don't you see? I love him."

Aaron was moved by her obvious pain.

"I know you're going through mourning."

"No. I'm not. You're denying it to me. I'm being denied my mourning. I can't have it until this is out of the way."

"Then let it end."

"Let it end for whom? A settlement ends it for you... for you and everybody else, but it keeps it from ending for me." Her voice broke again. "And the children. They'll grow up thinking their father..."

She could not go on any further.

"Wait a minute," Aaron said, "are you telling me that until you know he's innocent..."

Betsy interrupted him, angrily, "I KNOW he's innocent. Until YOU know it...and THEY know it...and everyone else!"

Aaron just stared at her. What could he say?

"Do you realize the cost?" he finally asked.

"I'll raise the money...somehow. I'll go back to work... I'll sell the house.."

"Forget about going back to work until you get your strength back. As for the house...it looks like you'll have to sell it anyway."

"I owe you a lot of money, too, don't I, Aaron? I know it cost a lot to go get the children, for which I will be eternally grateful."

"I can wait," he said waving his hand.

"So, what happens now?" asked Betsy.

"The Insurance Company will be wanting a deposition from you as soon as they receive the papers for the countersuit."

"What will that be like?"

"Much like the FBI interrogation."

"Well...I guess I can go through it again."

"They won't be as kind. It's their money at stake. Also, I hate to sound like a broken record but I must remind you again, it is imperative that you avoid reading about, or listening to, anything concerning Neil. Your belief in his innocence is our best weapon."

———

It was a small room with a bulletin board on one side and a blackboard on the other. There was a large artist's drawing of the plane exploding pinned on the bulletin board, recreated from the available evidence. It showed one man being blown out of the plane, and a shredded briefcase.

This was the FBI office where John O'Brien and Harry Carter sat at a table with their immediate superior,

Paul Hunter. Paul was a husky man in his 50's, strictly business. The table was strewn with papers and glossy black and white photographs of the plane's crashed cockpit, along with pictures of bodies.

John was trying to defend Betsy to Paul.

He said, "Paul, there's no way that girl murdered her husband."

"That's not for you to decide. Your job is to collate information on her," replied Paul.

"We haven't come up with one thing shady about her. She never even skipped school, for God's sake!"

"How many times does it turn out some crazy sniper was a model boy scout?" Paul retorted.

"Maybe we're overlooking something," John mused.

"Or, maybe she knows damn well he committed suicide and is covering up so she can collect a million dollars. You just keep on her tail," commanded Paul.

THIRTEEN

Betsy had made the decision to go back to work. She called Ellen, the head of the Model Agency, to tell her she was coming in to discuss returning. Ellen was on the phone with a client when Betsy arrived, but ended the call quickly with "Darling, I'll have to call you back." She plunked the phone down without waiting for a reply, and stood up with arms outstretched to greet Betsy, swept over and embraced her. Then held her at arm's length to examine her. In her machine gun style delivery, she addressed her.

"You're as beautiful as ever, and you're even thinner, that's good. It's marvelous that you're coming back to work. You couldn't have picked a better time. Two of my top models are pregnant. Can you start right away?"

"I guess so," said Betsy in a hesitant manner. "I've been out for over six months though. That's longer than I took off when I gave birth to my two kids. It'll be like starting all over."

"Nonsense!" said Ellen. "Everybody knows you. I'll put out a release announcing you're available again. They'll all be dying to see you."

"Oh, Ellen, I was kind of hoping to keep it quiet... maybe even change my name."

"Don't be silly, child! Do you want to make money or not.?"

Betsy did, so an arrangement was reached. After chatting a bit with the booking girls, she left the office. On the way to the elevator, she passed two men but did not pay them any attention. One was drinking at the water fountain, the other reading a newspaper so that his face was hidden. These men were the same two men who had showed up at the crash site in the black Mercedes.

Betsy entered the elevator, and as the doors were about to close, an arm was thrust between them. The doors opened again to admit the two Hispanic men. The elevator began its descent when suddenly one of the men reached over and pushed a button. The elevator jolted to a stop between floors, startling Betsy.

"What are you doing?" she asked.

One of the men replied, "Don't be alarmed, Mrs. Sanders. We just want to ask you a simple question. That's all."

"Oh, for Heaven's sake!" Don't you FBI people ever give up? What is it now?"

"We need to know who your husband was meeting in Miami."

"You already asked me that. I told you I don't remember his name. It sounded Spanish. That's all I remember."

"Would you recognize the name if you heard it?"

"Possibly."

"Could it have been Carl Rodriguez?"

"Yes! That's it," said Betsy, relieved. "Now would you mind starting the elevator? I've got a train to catch."

"Of course."

He pushed the button to restart the elevator.

Betsy muttered under her breath, "Unbelievable!"

———

The offices of Eastern Mutual Insurance Company were in a modern high-rise building on 5th Avenue. Aaron and Betsy took the elevator to the 12th floor and started down a long corridor. Her high heels beat a loud tattoo on the polished marble floor.

"Aaron, why did you tell me to wear the highest heels I had?"

"Psychological warfare. This guy is short, and I want us to be looking down on him."

"Oh, Aaron!" She laughed.

"You have absolutely nothing to be nervous about. Just stay cool, and only answer questions you're asked," Aaron counseled her.

"I have a few questions I'd like to ask THEM, such as why they sold that policy to Neil in the first place, if it's so abnormally large."

"We'll have our chance to ask questions later," Aaron reassured her.

When they arrived at Hank Beatty's luxurious corner office, there were four other men there in addition to Beatty. Two were lawyers with the firm. The others were Vince Tercasio and Wally Cooper of Nation Air. Also present was Hilda Bratton, a court stenographer. Beatty was playing the perfect host. He came from behind his massive oak desk and greeted Betsy first.

"Good afternoon, Mrs. Sanders. You're even more beautiful than your photographs." He then turned to the others. "Gentlemen, let me present Mrs. Neil Sanders and her Attorney, Aaron Ross." Then, to Aaron and Betsy, "This is Stuart Ferguson and Ron Miller, both with our office, and this is Vince Tercasio and Wally Cooper from Nation Air, whom I believe you've met, Aaron. They are joint claimants."

Everyone shook hands politely, muttering greetings.

"And last, but not least," Beatty continued, "this is our stenographer, Hilda Bratton."

Hilda nodded, poised over her machine. The ultimate in efficiency. As soon as everyone was seated, except Beatty, Hilda addressed Betsy:

"Would you raise your right hand, please?"

Betsy looked to Aaron who nodded. Betsy raised her hand.

"Do you swear to tell the truth, the whole truth, and nothing but the truth, so help you God?"

"I do," Betsy answered.

"You may lower your hand now," said Hilda.

Beatty slowly circled behind his desk, still standing, picked up a file folder. He studied it for a full twenty seconds, then put it down before addressing Betsy. He was on his game.

"Mrs. Sanders, Hilda will be taking down every word that is said. However, if there is anything you want to say off the record, just say, 'Can we go off the record,' and we will. We're not trying to harass you. Do you understand?"

"Yes, I think so," she answered.

"Okay, let's get right into it then. Mrs. Sanders, when did you first learn of Mr. Sander's insurance policy?"

"When the insurance agent came to the house to sell it to him," she replied.

"You were present at that time?"

"Yes, I was. And I told Neil later that I didn't like that salesman's tactics at all."

"What sort of tactics?" he inquired.

"He told Neil some ridiculous story about a friend of his who had died with no insurance, and his widow had to marry some rich, fat, old slob...his words, not mine... just so she and the children wouldn't starve. It was insulting and offensive."

"I'm sorry about that," said Beatty, "but to continue... why a million dollars?

"It was $500,000.   Not a million. That's what the salesman said he should have based on his projected income."

"You're saying the amount of the policy was decided by the salesman?"

"Yes. He told me if anything happened to Neil, I'd be the richest widow in town. I said, 'I don't want to be the richest widow in town.' I didn't like that man at all."

"In your opinion, did your husband give an honest assessment of his income?"

"Of course."

"But he neglected to mention to the salesman his impending disbarment."

"Disbarment!   What are you talking about?" she asked, glancing at Aaron, incredulously.

"Surely you knew he was under investigation by the Bar Association."

"I knew nothing of the sort!" she asserted.

"Mrs. Sanders, your husband took out this insurance shortly after that investigation began. It is our opinion that he knew he was in hot water, so deep there was no way out, and he chose to end his life rather than face disgrace and jail...masking his suicide as an accident so you could collect on the policy. What is your answer to that, Mrs. Sanders?"

"What was the question?"

Vince Tercasio concealed a smile behind his hand. Hank Beatty was visibly annoyed. He turned to Wally Cooper, and requested that he hand him a briefcase. Wally handed him the brown leather briefcase, which he in turn handed to Betsy with a question:

"Is this the type of briefcase your husband carried?" he asked.

"I guess so. I never examined it closely."

"What did he carry in it?"

"I don't know. I never opened it."

"Weren't you curious?"

"No. I had no reason to be."

Beatty took the briefcase from her and spoke as if he was drilling the words into her:

"Mrs. Sanders, a briefcase exactly like this one was carried aboard the plane. It was found in the vicinity of the crash site with the bottom blown out. Tests confirmed that it had contained explosive materials that took the lives of thirty-three innocent people."

He suddenly opened the case, reached into it, and produced a picture of mutilated bodies on the ground at the scene of the crash. He continued:

"A couple of them were little children."

Betsy turned her head, unable to look at the picture. Her eyes filled with tears.

"I know in my heart that Neil would never have done such a horrible thing," she protested.

"We have accumulated substantial evidence that leads us to believe that he did," Beatty countered.

He took a piece of paper from the briefcase and began to read slowly:

"The body was found twenty miles away from the main crash site, indicating he was closest to the source of the explosion. A sizable hole was in the flooring under the seat, and the metal tubular framework of the seat was violently distorted when it was recovered. An imprint of the fabric pattern of the seat was found on Mr. Sander's hips."

Betsy's closed her eyes in pain as he read on.

"Tiny fragments of metal were embedded in Mr. Sander's body that were not part of the plane, and both legs were severed below the knee in a manner reminiscent of the injuries produced by land mines in the war."

Aaron, sickened by the effect this was having on Betsy, interrupted the reading.

"Just a minute, Beatty. These descriptions are cruel and unnecessary."

Beatty replied, "I believe they are pertinent because Mrs. Sanders should be informed of all the reasons we believe her husband was responsible for blowing up that plane. Do you wish to stop and say anything off the record, Mrs. Sanders?"

"I just want to get this over with as quickly as possible," Betsy said.

"All right. Let me ask a few more questions then. Would your husband have known how to make a bomb?" he asked.

"I seriously doubt it," Betsy answered.

"He was in the Army, wasn't he? Perhaps he learned some wiring skills there."

"He didn't have any wiring skills."

"Didn't he ever help out around the house, repairing appliances, etc.?"

"No. He wasn't very handy that way."

At that moment, the phone rang. Beatty answered it.

"Beatty." He smiled, obviously pleased with what he heard on the other end of the line. "Splendid! Just what I was hoping for...Good work, Stan." He turned to Aaron with a self-satisfied look. "That was Stanley Arnold, one of our lawyers. You've been overruled by the Federal Court," he announced.

Aaron was stunned.

"What does that mean?" Betsy asked, confused.

"It means that your countersuit to stop us from suing you has been thrown out," Beatty said to her.

He shot Aaron a look of contemptuous victory.

"See you in court."

—

At home that evening, Betsy was looking in on the children. Lillian had put them to bed earlier. She bent over the crib to kiss Ana who was already asleep. She tiptoed out and went into Sven's room. His bed was empty. She called out to him, softly at first, then louder as she became alarmed.

"Sven? Sven! Where are you" Answer me!"

She looked in the bathroom. Empty. She started down the stairs, still calling out:

"Sven? Sven!"

She noticed the door to the basement ajar and a light from below. She started down.

"Sven, answer me! I know you're down there."

She heard Sven's voice. "Here I am."

He was sitting on the floor, under a table, the size of a ping pong table, upon which was a very elaborate Lionel electric train set. In addition to the train itself, there was a switching yard, tracks leading into a countryside, railroad crossing guards that raised up when the train passed, and a water tower. Betsy knelt down to look under it.

"What are you doing under there? You scared me silly," she scolded.

"I'm fixing my train, Daddy showed me how."

"Well, come to bed. You have no business being down here by yourself."

She glanced up at the underside of the table and saw a myriad of different colored wires entwined. Horror dawned on her as she stared. She'd said at the insurance office Neil knew nothing of wiring. She'd believed it.

———

Betsy had a terrifying dream that night. She dreamed she had gone to the closet and opened the door. She noticed a briefcase on the floor and picked it up. It was the same briefcase she had been shown in Hank Beatty's office. She placed it on the bed and opened it. The briefcase was filled with a jumble of colored wires like the ones she had seen under the train set. She jumped back with a scream.

She had screamed out loud and it woke her up. She was panic stricken. Her body was drenched with sweat, and she gasped for breath. She turned on the lamp and saw by the clock that it was 1:30 A.M. Could she call someone at that hour, she wondered. She picked up a piece of paper on the night table, studied it for a few moments, and dialed the number written on it.

"It's Betsy. I apologize for calling at this hour, but you said if I ever needed to talk, you'd be available, and I really need to talk."

John O'Brien came over in short order. He stopped to check in with the agent on surveillance duty before he entered the house. As he and Betsy were sitting in front of the fire, drinking hot chocolate, he let her pour out her feelings.

"I'm all mixed up," she said. "I thought I knew Neil so well. Now I'm wondering if I knew him at all. First there was the thing about his having a girlfriend, and today Mr. Beatty said some things that really shook me up. It was like we were talking about two different people. I've got to find out the truth."

"Haven't you talked to Aaron about it?" he asked.

"I tried to, and he just told me to forget it. But I can't forget it. Even my dreams won't let me. I'm scared."

"Are you afraid he might have done it?"

"I can't allow myself to think that. John, please tell me...does the FBI have anyone else under suspicion except Neil? You don't have to tell me who..."

John interrupted, "I know what you want to hear. You want me to nurture your belief in Neil's innocence. I can't do that."

"Have you even considered it? I think the FBI just wants an easy case. They're only pointing at him because of the insurance. That doesn't prove a thing."

"There are other reasons," John said uneasily, "his involvement..."

Betsy angrily retorted, "All lawyers have to deal with questionable characters. That's their business, isn't it?"

"You know who you're angry at? You're angry at Neil. Because he hasn't turned out to be who you thought he was."

"Don't play psychiatrist with me," she retorted. "If no one else will look for another person, I will."

"How do you propose to do that?" he asked.

"I'll hire a private investigator."

"Those guys charge a bloody fortune. Where're you going to get that kind of money?" he asked.

"To begin with, I'm going back to work. And then there's this." Betsy picked up a real estate listing from the coffee table and handed it to John.

There were photographs of several houses on the sheet, one being Betsy's. Her house had a big "SOLD" printed diagonally over the picture.

She said, "I'll have some money shortly. The house is in escrow, and I've found a little place to rent. I'm selling our sailboat, too."

"You've got a lot of guts, Lady, I'll say that," he said admiringly, "I wish there was something I could do to help."

"There is. Clear his name."

"You don't give up, do you?"

"I know Neil didn't do what they're saying...all those people...I don't want my children growing up thinking..."

Overcome by emotion, she stopped to pull herself together. Then she had a thought.

"By the way, has anyone talked with Carl Rodriguez yet?"

"Excuse me?"

"Carl Rodriguez. The man who was meeting Neil in Miami."

"I thought you said you didn't remember his name."

"I didn't at first. Then, when one of your guys mentioned it, it rang a bell."

"What do you mean 'one of our guys'?" he asked, confused.

"I'm talking about those two characters who trapped me in the elevator."

"Whoa! I think you'd better start from the beginning."

Betsy told John the whole story. He could hardly wait to relate the information to his superior, Paul Hunter.

FOURTEEN

A few days later, Betsy had a booking at Rawlings Studio. She entered with a jaunty step and a smile, carrying a satchel bag filled with cosmetics, high heels and costume jewelry. Tools of the trade.

"It's good to see you back, Honey," said Ron.

"Good to be back," answered Betsy.

Ron pointed to a rack of dresses at the side of the room.

"The emerald green one is yours. It'll go with your eyes. You're doing a double by the way. The other model is in the dressing room."

"Francine?" she asked.

"No, I got a red-head this time."

Betsy took the dress off the rack and started toward the dressing room.

Ron called after her, "I'll give you girls five minutes for makeup. That's all I can afford at your prices."

Betsy entered the dressing room. The other model, dressed in a half slip and bra was brushing her beautiful red hair at the dressing table. She looked vaguely familiar, but no one she'd worked with before. Betsy's nose told her they wore the same perfume though. Shalimar.

She hung the green dress on a hook on the wall and introduced herself.

"Hi, I'm Betsy Sanders."

The other model did not respond at first. Betsy started doing her makeup and became aware that the girl was staring at her through the mirror. Betsy turned and asked,

"Is something wrong?"

The model answered her this time, still looking through the mirror as she spoke.

"I'm Sky Blue."

Betsy made a streak with her eyeliner, right up to her hairline. Now it was her time to stare. They looked at each other through the mirror, not moving. Sky looked sick.

"I guess you know."

Betsy did not answer. Sky put her head down on the dressing room table to hide her face.

"Oh, God."

Ron called out from the Studio, "You girls almost ready?"

"Almost," Betsy answered.

She wiped off the eyeliner and hastily applied lipstick, with which she had a little trouble because she kept glancing at Sky through the mirror. Neither actually looked at the other except through the mirror. Sky repaired some smudged mascara and met Betsy's eyes in the mirror.

"I don't know what to say. Do you want me to leave? What should I do?"

Betsy quickly unzipped her dress and slipped out of it. She was also clad in a half slip and bra. She answered Sky while taking the green dress off the hanger.

"Better get into your dress."

———

At a coffee shop a while later, Betsy and Sky sat opposite each other in a booth. Neither was paying much attention to the coffee in front of them. The cups were half empty. A waitress stopped by to top them off. Sky nervously tore a sugar wrapper into tiny pieces. Betsy broke the silence.

"I don't usually drink more than one cup of coffee a day."

"Me, either," said Sky. "I switch to decaf later."

"Is Sky Blue your real name?" asked Betsy.

"Yes, it really is, and would you believe I have a sister named True?"

"True Blue! You're kidding."

"My parents are kind of weird," said Sky, "it's one of the things I like about them." A pause followed that exchange, and then there was a collision as they both began to speak at the same time.

"I just want..."

"I know you..."

"Excuse me,. Go ahead."

"No, you first."

So Sky began. "I don't know how to say this...but, I'm sorry...for everything."

"Thanks. I'm sure this is hard on you, too. Funny...I never thought I'd be feeling sympathy for you."

"People feel a lot of things they never thought they'd feel," said Sky.

"Do you mind telling me how you and Neil met?"

"He gave me his card at a party."

"The Viennese Opera Ball?"

"Yes, how did you know?"

"I saw him talking to you."

"Oh. Anyway, I put the card in my evening bag and forgot about it. Months later I was having a problem with my landlord and I needed a lawyer. I remembered him, so I made a phone call. He suggested he come to my place instead of my going to his office. That was fine with me. He really did help me and then he didn't want to charge me a fee, so I invited him for dinner. I made coc au vin."

"That is funnier than you can imagine."

"Why?"

"Long story. Never mind. How often did you see each other?"

"Usually one afternoon a week, schedules permitting. Are you sure you want to hear this?" Sky asked.

"Actually I do, because I cannot for the life of me figure out why I never suspected anything, or why no one else said anything. Once a college friend of mine was visiting and I wasn't feeling well so Neil took her out to dinner. The next day it was in a gossip column that he was seen having dinner in a night club with a pretty blonde, not his wife. We had a good laugh over it."

"We never went anywhere in public," Sky volunteered.

"The FBI said you sometimes went on business trips with him."

"Sometimes we would drive to the Jersey shore for a couple of days. Someone he knew had a house there and would let Neil borrow it. I never met the person and don't know his name. It's so creepy knowing we were being spied on. Oh God, I feel so rotten about this now. Can you ever forgive me?"

"Yes. I believe in forgiveness. I admit I'm having a more difficult time forgiving Neil though. He's the one who made a vow to be faithful to me."

"I don't know how I let myself get involved with a married man."

"Were you in love with him?"

Sky nodded her head, yes. "I was captivated by him."

"Was he in love with you?"

"I wanted to believe he was, but he was committed to his marriage. He made that very clear, right from the beginning."

"I was wondering if you happened to talk with him the night he..."

She could not say the words.

"Yes," Sky answered, "He called me about midnight. He seemed nervous."

"He was always nervous about flying."

"I know. I thought maybe he'd change his mind about going, especially when he gave up his seat on the first flight. If he hadn't done that he'd be alive now."

"What do you mean, 'gave up his seat'?"

"You know they divided the flight into two planes, don't you?" Sky asked.

"Yes, of course." said Betsy.

"He told me he was scheduled to go on the first one, but he traded places with an old lady."

"Why would he do that?" Betsy asked.

"Her daughter was in the hospital in Miami and she was frantic to get there. He felt sorry for her."

"Did you tell this to the FBI when they questioned you?"

"It never came up. They were asking me more personal questions. Why? Do you think it's important?"

—

The next evening John O'Brien was seated in a booth at Spumoni's. He'd been surprised when Betsy called and asked to meet him there. He wondered what she wanted, hoping it might be him. His mind went back to the night she had called him at 1:30 in the morning and he had gone over. He thought about how she had looked her in her fleece robe and big fur slippers that reminded him of Minnie Mouse. She was not wearing any make up and her skin was glowing in the firelight. He had had such an urge to take her in his arms and make love to her right there, but it was obvious the only thing on her mind was Neil. It was as if his ghost was sitting between them.

Betsy came in, looked around, spotted John and hurried over, out of breath. She slid into the booth as John was rising to greet her. Without pausing she launched into her excuse for keeping him waiting talking a mile a minute with no commas.

"I'm sorry I'm late the job ran over there was this nutty client who wanted umpteen variations on every shot I hate it when the clients are on the set they can drive you crazy the lasagna here is to die for I'm starved." She took a breath, "How about you?"

"How do you do that?"

"What?"

He just laughed, and said, "I've never been here before. How do you know it?"

"It's an old favorite of mine and...of mine."

A waiter came to the table with a basket of bread and a saucer of olive oil. Addressing John, he asked if they would like something to drink. John looked at Betsy.

"Wine?" he asked.

"Perfect!" she answered.

"Shall we go ahead and order that lasagna you mentioned?"

"Sure."

"Two orders of lasagna, mixed green salads and a bottle of chianti." he said to the waiter.

"Yes Sir," And, the waiter departed.

"I like a man who takes charge," said Betsy.

"I was surprised when you invited me for dinner. Is it because I'm so charming, or do you have an ulterior motive?" John asked.

"Boy! You really do have a suspicious nature. Why would you even ask me something like that?"

"Voice of experience."

"I met Sky Blue," she blurted.

John let that sink in. Then, "Really? How did that happen?"

"We were on the same booking yesterday, and then we had coffee afterwards."

"Wasn't that a bit awkward?"

"It was at first, but we had an interesting talk."

"I think I'm about to find out why you called me," he teased.

"I need to talk to you."

The waiter came with the wine and poured each a glass.

"Okay. At least it's not two o'clock in the morning. Talk to me."

"Sky told me that Neil was supposed to be on the first flight but he gave up his seat to a woman who was going to see her daughter in the hospital."

"That was very gentlemanly of him," John commented.

Betsy reached for her wine and picked up the glass. Her hand was shaking. John put his hand on hers and lowered it.

"Take it easy," he said gently.

"I want to speak with her. Is there any way I can get that passenger list?"

"Afraid not."

"What's the harm? It would help bring me some closure."

"I'd certainly like for you to have closure..."

"Then..."

"I would get in a lot of trouble if I got involved."

"I sensed you were already somewhat involved," Betsy murmured, looking down.

"You're referring to my feelings. I can't operate on my feelings."

"How about my feelings?" she said, facing him directly.

"Betsy, I can't... but... there may be another way."

——

Betsy could not wait to follow John's advice. As soon as she arrived home, later that evening, she called Aaron at home. He did not take her discovery seriously.

"Aaron! I can't believe you're discounting this. John said you could get a court order to obtain the passenger list."

"Oh, it's 'John' now is it?" he said, dryly, "Assuming we find this woman, if she even exists, what could she tell us?"

"I don't know! You won't even try!" Betsy charged.

"Betsy, It's late. We're already in bed. And, you're beginning to try my patience. This sounds like a wild goose chase. Furthermore, to be perfectly frank, I've extended myself financially as far as I can. I'm not a big corporation."

"Could I at least come in and talk to you in person?" she pleaded.

Aaron, with a mixture of anger and guilt, agreed.

"Okay," he said, "if you can be in my office by eight in the morning. But Betsy...it's going to take more than talk. I have a lot on my plate right now."

———

Betsy got up at the crack of dawn the next morning so she could catch the early commuter to New York. She boarded the crowded train with all the regular commuters. She had to walk through several cars looking for a seat, subjecting herself to curious stares from other passengers. When she reached the smoke-filled Bar car, she spotted the only empty seat, next to a very expensively and flashily dressed man. She took it.

The man fate put her beside was Mel Friedman. He had thick, black wavy hair and wore large gold cuff links and a diamond ring. No sooner had Betsy sat down and unbuttoned her coat, when he spoke to her.

"Good morning," he said.

"Good morning."

"It's warming up a little don't you think?" he asked.

"Yes, it seems to be," she answered.

"I haven't seen you on this train before." he commented.

"I usually take a later train when I go in."

"Going into the city for a little shopping and lunch with the girls?" he inquired.

"I wish. No, I have an appointment with my lawyer," Betsy explained.

"Don't tell me a beautiful girl like you is going through a divorce."

"No. My husband was killed recently in a plane crash."

"How terrible! Was it the plane that was blown up by a bomb?"

"Yes."

"Oh, my God...you're...oh, I'm so sorry. Please forgive me. I saw your picture in the paper with your children, and it broke my heart."

"Not everyone felt that way. I've been shunned by half the town," said Betsy.

"No! That's awful! I wish there were some way I could help," he said, sympathetically.

Betsy did not respond at first. Could she really ask a stranger the question she had in mind? She decided to take a chance, and blurted out an unusual request.

"Would you lend me a thousand dollars?"

"What did you say?" he stammered.

"I'll pay it back...well, maybe I won't be able to, but I think I will. If I collect the insurance...I will."

Friedman looked at her in complete astonishment. His first impulse was to refuse her. Then his curiosity got the better of him.

"A thousand dollars is a lot of money. Why do you need it?" he asked.

"Because the insurance company is suing me," she told him.

"That's incredible! What do you mean they're suing you? How can they do that? What for?"

Betsy told him the whole story, leaving out nothing.

In the meantime, while she was talking to Friedman, the four card players, Fred, Al, Joe and Charlie, were watching them.

"Do you see who she's talking to? That guy's a pimp," said Charlie.

"How would you know that, Charlie," asked Joe.

"Never mind. I know. I thought you said she was an innocent little country girl, Fred."

"Charlie," said Fred, impatiently, "she sat there because there was an empty seat. She's just talking to him, for Christ's sake!"

"Well, pardon me."

"Hey, c'mon guys," Joe interjected, "are we playing or not?"

They returned their attention to the game. Friedman, meanwhile was nodding his head trying to understand the story Betsy was telling him. It was a tough one to follow.

Betsy concluded by saying, "So if I win the case, I'll pay you back DOUBLE, but if I lose, I won't be able to pay you back at all. Oh...never mind. It was a crazy idea."

"Not so fast" Friedman said, "I don't know why, but I'm going to take a gamble."

"Wha...? Oh, THANK you! You're a wonderful, kind man! I just realized I don't even know your name," Betsy gushed.

"Mel. Mel Friedman...here," he took out a piece of paper and a gold pen. "I don't walk around with that kind of cash on me, but if you'll meet me in my barber shop at two o'clock, I'll have the money for you. Here's the address." He wrote on the slip of paper and handed it to Betsy.

"You own a barbershop?"

"No, Honey. I'm a customer."

Charlie happened to look up just as Betsy took the piece of paper. He smiled knowingly and nudged Fred, saying, "Just talking, huh?"

———

When Betsy got to Aaron's office and told him what she had done, he was appalled.

"If you really believe he's going to be there, then you're even more naïve than I thought," Aaron said.

"He was a very nice man, and I could tell he had money by the way he was dressed. He even wore a diamond ring," Betsy answered.

"Oh, God, Betsy! When are you going to grow up?"

"I'm going to find that woman and talk to her," Betsy asserted.

"That's going to take some doing. Tell me exactly why you want to talk to her."

"Because she's the last person I know of who spoke to Neil, She may have seen or heard something."

"You're wasting your time. I really wish you wouldn't pursue this."

"What is it going to hurt if I just talk to her? What is it you're not saying?" she asked.

"If it does turn out to be true that Neil exchanged seats with someone, it could possibly work against you."

"How? I don't understand."

Aaron looked down. He could not meet her eyes as he delivered his next statement.

"It's common knowledge that most people who commit suicide stall if off for a while, when it gets right down to it."

Betsy was shocked. She was unable to deal with that possibility and was furious that Aaron would even consider it.

"Aaron, I'm going to pretend I didn't even hear that."

She left the building, still fuming. The logic of what Aaron told her was devastating. She was so upset she didn't look where she was going and bumped square into John O'Brien. She was so on edge, she boiled over at the sight of him.

"Every time I turn around you're there. Are you following me?"

Then she saw he was holding out an envelope.

"What's this?" she asked.

"Do you have to ask?"

She stared at the envelope without taking it.

"This is what you wanted," John said, "the passenger list."

She reached out and took the envelope. Impulsively she threw her arms around him. Startled, he held her for a moment, then both drew back, embarrassed. She hurried off. It was just that her emotions were all in a turmoil she told herself. It didn't mean anything. Still, she couldn't help thinking how good it felt to have a man's arms around her again. He smelled good, too. Irish Spring, she guessed.

———

Rudy's barbershop was located in a small hotel in the 50's, on the west side of Manhattan. He was a popular barber with the show biz crowd. He knew everybody, and liked to brag about it. As he was in the process of cutting Mel Friedman's hair he was on a roll.

"Paul Newman was in the other day. I always cut his hair, you know, except when he's on the coast. He says I'm better than Sassoon."

"Who cares about Paul Newman," replied Friedman, "let me know when you do Marilyn Monroe."

"Have you ever seen his eyes?" Rudy asked.

"Have you ever seen her ass?" Friedman countered.

Through the mirror, Rudy caught sight of Betsy standing in the doorway. He turned around and asked, "Can I help you, Miss?"

Friedman turned around and saw her, too. He said, "Over here, Betsy. Come on in."

Betsy walked tentatively over to the chair.

"I wasn't sure you'd be here, Mr. Friedman," she said.

"It's Mel."

"Mel."

"I'm a man of my word."

He opened his wallet and counted out ten one hundred dollar bills into her hand. Rudy watched open-mouthed.

"I can't thank you enough," Betsy gushed, "you're just wonderful. Thank you."

"Well, that's a first!" observed Rudy.

Betsy started toward the door, hesitated awkwardly. Friedman gave her a little wave.

"Good luck," he called out.

"Did I just see what I think I saw?" asked Rudy.

"I don't know...what do you think you saw, Rudy?"

"I think I just saw you give some gal a thousand dollars."

"Nah, you're imagining things."

———

Charlie and Al boarded the afternoon train together. While they were passing through one of the cars on the way to the Bar Car, Charlie happened to see Betsy seated by a window, an empty seat beside her. He said to Al, "you go on ahead. Save my seat."

"What're you doing," Al growled, "you're going to louse up the game."

"Tough!"

Charlie brushed his hair back with his fingers, and straightened his tie. He turned on his most charming smile as he approached Betsy.

"Pardon me, is this seat taken?" inquired Charlie.

"No, it isn't," she replied.

Al threw Charlie an exasperated look as he saw him sit down beside Betsy. He then headed on to the Bar Car.

Fred and Joe entered the car shortly after and took their usual seats, putting a briefcase on Charlie's seat to save his place.

"He's wasting his time," Fred said.

"I don't know," said Joe, "he's a pretty good operator. I've watched him."

"Wait and see," replied Fred.

After a brief period of time, Charlie appeared at their side with a very strange look on his face.

"What's the matter, Charlie?" asked Fred, amused, guessing what it was.

"You won't believe what that woman asked me!" Charlie sputtered.

FIFTEEN

It was a dismal, gray, rainy day in New York. The taxi pulled up outside an ancient apartment building on the lower East side. Betsy, in the back seat, sat looking at the raindrops rolling down the window. She made no move to get out. After a few moments, the driver turned around to speak to her.

"This is the address you gave me, Lady. Are you getting out or not?"

She paid the driver, exited the taxi, and quickly ducked into the building. The smell of chicken cooking was heavy in the air. She walked up two flights of stairs and found the apartment number she was looking for. She knocked on the door.

Mrs. Epstein, a wiry, birdlike woman, opened the door a crack and peered out. Her eyes, behind steel-rimmed spectacles, were sharp.

"Are you Mrs. Epstein?" Betsy asked.

"Yes, what is it?"

"I'm Betsy Sanders. It was my husband, Neil, who traded places with you on the flight to Miami."

Mrs. Epstein did not respond. Betsy continued:

"Mrs. Epstein, could I please come in and talk to you for a few minutes?"

"Why do you want to talk to me?"

"You were the last person I know of who spoke to my husband before he died...please?" Betsy implored.

Mrs. Epstein opened the door for her to come in.

The furnishings were old, but tasteful. A few fine pieces. The room was as neat as a pin. Many photographs filled every available table. Betsy was drawn to a framed photograph of a handsome five-year old boy, holding a puppy. She looked at it a moment and then turned her attention to Mrs. Epstein.

"I heard that your daughter was in the hospital. Is she all right now?" she asked.

"She's coming along," Mrs. Epstein said. "She had a stroke. Went down for a vacation, and had a stroke."

"I'm so sorry."

"Thank you...I'm sorry for your loss." There was a pause and then Mrs. Epstein said, "Sit down. Would you like some tea?"

"Thank you, not right now," Betsy replied.

Betsy could hardly wait to get to why she had come. As soon as she was seated, she leaned forward and began.

"Mrs. Epstein, can you tell me about your conversation with my husband? How did you happen to talk to him?"

"He was talking to my grandson," Mrs. Epstein answered.

"Your grandson?"

"That's him," she pointed to a picture. "The one you were looking at. He's five years old."

"He's a beautiful boy. I have a five-year old boy, too," Betsy said.

"I know you do," Mrs. Epstein replied. A pause hovered in the air, and she added, "Your husband told me."

"Neil talked about the children?"

"Well, he was really talking to Martin. He told him he had a boy his age."

Betsy was listening attentively.

"Was Martin with you on the plane?" she inquired.

"Of course."

"You mean they had put you and your grandson on different planes?"

"No. We were together. We were assigned the second plane, but your husband gave up his seat for me."

"But...then someone else had to change places with Martin," Betsy ventured.

"That's right," said Mrs. Epstein, "the fellow who was with your husband traded with him. He didn't want to at first, but your husband talked him into it."

"My husband was traveling alone," Betsy protested.

"I was in the same waiting room with them for over three hours. I ought to know."

"I didn't mean to contradict..."

"I watched everything they did because Martin was talking to them. Your husband got a coco cola for himself and Martin, and the other fellow got a coffee. They always held onto their briefcases, never set them down, even when they went to make a phone call."

"Did they both make phone calls?" asked Betsy.

"That's right."

"What happened while they were making the calls?"

"Nothing happened. Did I say something happened?"

"You mentioned they were holding something."

"Oh, their briefcases. They both had nice brown, leather briefcases."

Betsy drew a deep breath and said, slowly, "They both had nice brown, leather briefcases...Mrs. Epstein, if the offer still holds, I think I'd like that tea now."

———

In the FBI office the next day, Paul Hunter was chewing John O'Brien out. He was furious.

"Damn it, John! You had no right getting involved in a private investigation. It's none of your business. What's more, what you did is illegal."

"Look, our job is to find out who blew up that plane," John replied. "All I did was get her the passenger list. She did the leg work. Frankly, I'm very impressed at what she came up with."

"You've fallen for her and you're being irrational! I've got half a mind to transfer you to Alaska!" barked Paul. "I warned you about that when you made that after hours visit."

"Hey, that was productive. We found out about Carl Rodriguez, didn't we?"

"Yeah, too late. Too bad she didn't remember his name when you first interviewed her. Unfortunately dead men don't talk. Whatever happened to those two guys ?"

"They apparently left town after they got the information they wanted. Tell me something. Who was sitting beside Neil Sanders in the plane?" John asked.

Paul looked over at Harry Carter, but didn't need to verbalize the request. Harry was already consulting the files.

"The C.A.B. has a George Gonzales seated beside Sanders," Harry said.

John pounced on that. "That's a phony name if I ever heard one."

Paul looked at him, and shook his head in disgust.

Harry, who was still looking at the report, asked John, "Did she get a description on this Gonzales guy?"

"Latin-looking. Dark curly hair, olive skin, moustache, in his early forties. Short. Stocky. Wore tinted glasses."

"Nothing in here about the glasses, but the rest fits," said Harry. "He was Cuban."

"That's a very observant old lady," admitted Paul.

"She was even able to describe their briefcases. They both had brown leather briefcases," John added.

Paul made a note of that. "That's important. Who claimed Gonzales's body, Harry?" he asked.

"His landlady identified it. They put an announcement in the papers to notify his family, but nobody showed up, so the State buried him," Harry said.

"How in hell did we miss this?" Paul fumed. "Get what you can on this guy, Gonzales, and I want the body exhumed and autopsied." He turned to John. "Don't think this means you're off the hook."

"It never entered my mind," said John.

———

Following the exhumation of George Gonzales, and subsequent investigation, John O'Brien briefed Aaron on their findings in preparation for his meeting with the Insurance Company to go over the new evidence. Aaron asked John how much of the information he thought the Insurance Company might already know.

"I have no idea," John said, "why do you ask?"

"Beatty insists that I bring Betsy to the meeting, and I'd like to keep some of the more lurid details from her. It's going to kill her to hear all this."

"I don't see how you're going to make your case and keep it from her. Don't go in with one hand tied behind your back," said John.

"You're right. I wish you weren't, but you are," Aaron admitted.

———

Betsy and Aaron were back in Hank Beatty's plush corner office. Wally Cooper, of Nation Air, was sitting in the corner, silent, but paying rapt attention. Betsy, seated next to Aaron, was pitched forward listening. Her pulse was racing and her eyes were on Hank Beatty as Aaron was speaking to him.

"According to the FBI, passenger George Gonzales is actually Angel Rosales, a minor member of the Cuban Mafia. We have an eye witness who says Rosales was also carrying a brown leather briefcase."

"Why wasn't that briefcase found?" asked Beatty.

"We believe that's the one, or what was left of it, that WAS found in the vicinity of the crash," answered Aaron.

"If that's so, where is Sanders' case?"

"Neil Sanders' case may have been removed from the wreckage. There were reports that two unidentified men appeared at the site, asking permission to search for some papers. His case may have been full of money, and they could have taken it."

"That's ridiculous!" interrupted Wally Cooper, "the site was sealed."

"This was the morning of the crash," said Aaron. "It hadn't been established there was a bomb involved, and security wasn't yet a priority. It was a zoo there. I heard the red necks were swarming like bees."

"Show me the briefcase, and I'll listen," challenged Beatty.

Betsy started to speak, but was stopped by Aaron's hand on her arm. She settled back in her chair, her face reflecting pain as she listened to Aaron's next statement.

"There's more," said Aaron. "Both of Angel's legs were blown off, too, and his body was permeated with the same bits of metal Neil Sanders body was."

"How do you know that?" Beatty asked.

"The FBI exhumed the body."

"But Sanders was blown out of the plane before it crashed," argued Beatty.

"All that proves is that he was sitting by the window, which, according to the FAA, he was. Angel was blown into the interior of the plane," explained Aaron.

"The bomb was most probably between them, under the seat."

"I believe their facts are correct on that point," interjected Wally Cooper.

Beatty glared at Cooper. "If you don't mind, I'm handling this." Turning back to Aaron he said, "So, that could have been Sander's case."

"Or it could just as well have been Angel Rosales's case."

"You don't know that."

"It certainly raises reasonable doubt as to whose briefcase it was."

"What about motive? What reason did Angel have for committing suicide? Sanders had plenty," Beatty countered.

This angered Betsy and she was about to speak. Once more Aaron stopped her. He continued:

"I don't think it was suicide at all. Angel had a noon reservation to Venezuela the following day. As you probably know, the Cuban Mafia has been running a ton of money down there."

"Yes, I'm aware of that. So what?" asked Beatty. "That's Castro's problem."

"Our theory, mine and the FBI's, is that Angel thought he was carrying money, as Sanders probably was, but a bomb had been substituted."

"In other words, you think he was a hit victim. For what reason?"

"Since when does the Mafia operate on reason?" asked Aaron. "Their moral codes would shock the most corrupt cop in New York. These guys would shoot their best friend at point blank range if their boss ordered it."

The idea of Neil being involved with the Mafia was really getting to Betsy. She dug her nails into her palm to try to keep her face from crumbling.

"This is all speculation," said Beatty arrogantly. "You have no real motive for Mr. Rosales's suicide or murder."

"I'm quite confident that the court will find we've raised more than a reasonable doubt as to Neil Sanders' guilt," said Aaron.

Hank Beatty, aware of the impact this was having on Betsy, decided to try another tack.

"Counselor, I'm well aware that you do not wish to subject your client to a court trial," He smiled sympathetically at Betsy. "I don't blame you. She has suffered enough. In view of this, perhaps I can persuade my colleagues to grant Mrs. Sanders some sort of compensation."

Betsy's head came up at this and her eyes flashed. She looked at Aaron.

"What sort of compensation did you have in mind?" Aaron asked.

"I didn't have anything in mind. Off the top of my head though...I think a hundred thousand would be more than fair."

"You're out of your gourd, Beatty!" Aaron said.

Something in Betsy was boiling over. She could no longer keep quiet.

"Just a minute!" she said angrily.

They all reacted with surprise at her outburst. She looked them over and continued. "I want to go to court."

They stared at her and she met their gazes. Something was rising in her that she couldn't keep in.

"If the Cuban Mafia killed this Angel person, I don't see how it involves Neil at all! Let the court settle it," she demanded.

Hank Beatty had not expected this, but he still had some weapons. He faced Aaron.

"You really have protected your client, haven't you, Aaron? Well, perhaps it's time she was told the facts of life." He turned to Betsy. "Then we'll see if you still want to go to court, Mrs. Sanders."

He got up on his feet and continued to talk before Aaron could interrupt. He paced before Betsy as though addressing a jury. Betsy never took her eyes off him.

"Neil Sanders was involved all right. He was negotiating a placement of underworld funds in Venezuela."

"Venezuela...Neil?" Betsy asked, horrified.

"That's right, Mrs. Sanders. He and a man named Carl Rodriguez, who was the Vice President of a large bank in Venezuela, had a scheme of their own going. You don't double-cross these people. Rodriguez 'accidently' drowned in Biscayne Bay one night...he'd been drinking, and fell off a yacht was the story."

Betsy's stomach dropped. She had given those two men Carl Rodriguez's name that day in the elevator. Beatty let his last statement sink in, then addressed Betsy again.

"That's not all..." he began to continue.

Betsy stood up. "I have to leave for a few minutes," she said, "I think I'm going to be sick."

Aaron tried to take her arm when she stood but she pushed it away.

"I'll take you," he said.

"I can find it myself," Betsy answered sharply.

When the door closed behind her, Aaron looked at Beatty. He could hardly contain his fury.

"Was that really necessary?" he asked.

"She ain't heard nothin' yet. I'm going to hit her with every low-down dirty thing her husband ever did. If she can't take it now, how's she going to like it in court? I'm at my best there," taunted Beatty.

"Beatty, you don't want to go to court any more than I do," said Aaron.

"You got a solution?" Beatty asked.

"Five-hundred thousand, the face amount of the policy," Aaron stated authoritatively.

"Now who's out of their gourd?" Beatty retorted. "But just to show you I'm as compassionate as the next guy though, I'll double my original offer. Two hundred thousand."

"You know damn well the court will award us at least five," Aaron contended.

"Maybe they will, and maybe they won't. Do you really want to take that chance?" asked Beatty.

Aaron thought it over. "Let me have a word with her." He left the office.

After Aaron went out, Wally Cooper and Beatty exchanged a look of satisfaction.

"Good going," said Wally. "I think we have them."

When Betsy came out of the ladies room, Aaron was waiting for her in the corridor. He put his arm around her. She pushed it away.

"Are you all right?" he asked.

"No, I am not all right," Betsy retorted. "I'm going to ask you something, and I want an honest answer. I don't want you protecting me anymore. Were those things he said about Neil true or not? Was he really involved with the Cuban Mafia? I didn't even know there was such a thing."

Aaron took a deep breath before responding. "There is such a thing all right. They own all the gambling casinos down there. And, yes...I'm sorry to tell you... everything he said about Neil is true. Furthermore, he's going to hit you with a lot more if you go back in there. You don't have to hear it...listen...I got him to double the offer. Two hundred thousand. I strongly advise you to take it."

"This is either a bad dream, or I'm a very poor judge of character. I should have noticed something. Mr. Beatty mentioned Venezuela. Neil took me to Caracas on a vacation once. Everyone said, 'why are you going there in summer, it'll be so hot?' but it wasn't. The weather was perfect. It's called the 'City of red roofs' you know, because of all the red tile roofs."

"You must have had to fly to get there. What about Neil's phobia?" asked Aaron.

"It's the only vacation we ever took where we had to fly. Neil got the doctor to give him some tran-quilizers...Miltown I think they were called. He was determined to go there. I didn't question it. I was just glad to be going somewhere with him. We stayed in a fabulous hotel with a beautiful swimming pool and spa. We couldn't go out at night because there was a lot of crime there and Neil said it would be dangerous. The hotel had a casino though, and I played roulette while Neil played cards with some men. Now I'm wondering who those men were. I never asked any questions. Was I being used as a cover? How could I have been so stupid!"

"Don't be so hard on yourself. You were very young when you met Neil. He dazzled you. And, you're not the only one. I've been a friend of the family since Neil was a boy. His father was my mentor, for God's sake! He fooled us all. I'm as shocked as you are."

"Somehow I doubt that," said Betsy. "But, I have another question...do you think Neil was murdered?"

"It's possible," Aaron said. "There's also the possibility that the bomb was meant for Rodriguez in Miami. We learned that there was a plot to assassinate two high-ranking members of the Mafia. He could very well have been one of them, and the flight's being delayed could have loused up the timing."

"In which case Neil's death would have been accidental," said Betsy.

"Right. We'd have to prove it though, and frankly we haven't a prayer. Take the two hundred thousand," he implored. "It'll pay some of your debts."

When Aaron and Betsy reentered Beatty's office, Betsy took her chair and looked him in the eye.

"All right, Mr. Beatty. Do you want to continue, or do you want to save yourself for the trial?"

Beatty was stunned. He looked to Aaron for an explanation. Aaron could hardly believe it himself. He looked at Betsy admiringly as he addressed Beatty.

"She won't accept your offer. She wants to go to court for the whole million. Accidental death."

"Why do you want to do that, Mrs. Sanders?" Beatty asked.

"Because no matter what else my husband may have been guilty of, he would NEVER have blown up a plane load of people. Only by your paying the full amount of the policy will that blame be removed from him."

"If your husband was murdered because of his involvement with the underworld, doesn't that make him equally responsible.?"

"No. It doesn't," said Betsy.

"Are you aware that murder is not considered an accident?" asked Beatty.

"But you will have to prove he was murdered, won't you?" she said.

"You WANT me to prove he was murdered? If we do, then you certainly would not be able to collect double indemnity. Murder is not considered an accident."

"Yes, I heard you the first time. But, if it's proved he was murdered, it proves he didn't blow up the plane. Or...as my attorney pointed out to me, Carl Rodriguez could have been the real target. I mean they did kill him, didn't they? That's what you implied. And, if that's the case, Neil's death would have been... accidental."

"You'd owe her one million dollars," said Aaron.

"You'd be willing to go through a trial, and possibly end up with even less than we've offered you?" asked Beatty.

"A good name is to be chosen rather than great riches," said Betsy

"Jesus Christ!," said Beatty, looking at her as though she was crazy.

"No, it's from Proverbs," said Betsy.

Beatty pondered the situation. He didn't like what he was about to say, but maybe he could close the deal and still save face. He addressed Betsy again.

"Oh Lord!...Mrs. Sanders, your attorney suggested we pay you the face amount of the policy. Would you be willing to accept that, if it were offered that is?"

"On one condition?" replied Betsy.

"Which is?"

"You get the charges against Neil dropped."

This was too much. Beatty was thrown by her request. It was more than he bargained for. He looked over at Wally Cooper, who remained impassive.

"You understand," he said, "I'm not making you that offer. I'm only asking if you would accept the offer if it was made."

"And, I'm not accepting the offer that you're not making. I'm just telling you the conditions under which I would accept it...if it was made."

———

After Aaron and Betsy had left Hank Beatty's office, the two men sat in silence for a few moments, each mulling over what had just transpired.

Then Wally asked, "Just out of curiosity, why didn't you take her up on her request to go to court instead of talking settlement?"

"I'll tell you why, and this is just between us," said Beatty.

"Okay."

"A friend of mine in Massachusetts, who shall remain nameless, told me that Sanders might have been going down to Miami to turn State's evidence."

"You think it's true?"

"I don't know if it's true or not, and we never WILL know. But if even the possibility of it is raised...."

"I get it," Wally interrupted, "it would undercut your claim of suicide."

"Right. They already have enough for reasonable doubt. This would be icing on the cake."

"I do think we might be able to negotiate for a lower amount though," Wally said.

"Lower? I intend to cut it in HALF!"

"Now there's the Fred Beatty I know and love," said Wally with a smile.

———

———

The bar car had already started to do business although the afternoon train hadn't even left Grand Central Station yet. Everyone was already in a weekend mode. On the train, Fred held up the Daily News for his buddies to see.

"Have you seen this?"

'AIRLINE DROPS CHARGES AGAINST SANDERS. NEW EVIDENCE IMPLICATES CUBAN MAFIA'

"I told you so," he crowed.

"Here comes the millionairess now," Charlie said.

"She didn't get a million dollars, Charlie," said Fred.

At that moment, Betsy was entering the car. She looked stunning. By then, many of the passengers felt as if they knew her. They smiled and spoke to her in a friendly way. She seemed to have captured the hearts of everyone. The card playing group watched as she walked through the car, nodding and accepting words of congratulation.

They saw her stop beside Mel Friedman, who was seated in an aisle seat. They watched as Betsy and Friedman engaged in animated conversation. Then she reached into her big model's bag and retrieved a fat envelope, which she handed to Friedman. When she reached the card group she greeted them cheerily. Again, she reached into her bag and pulled out two more fat envelopes. She gave these to Fred and Charlie. They looked at each other sheepishly, opened the envelopes and grinned.

"What the Hell?" exclaimed Al.

Fred explained to Joe and Al what the envelopes were all about.

"I can't believe you guys went for that," said Joe.

"What I can't believe is that she really paid us back double," replied Charlie.

"I know. I feel like giving it back to her," said Fred.

"Save it and give it to her for a wedding present when she gets married again," suggested Charlie.

Betsy had gone on past. Seated at the end of the car, was John O'Brien. She slid gracefully into the empty seat beside him, and said flirtatiously, "Why, Agent O'Brien, are you still following me? What are you looking for now?"

When their eyes met it was obvious what he was looking for, and that he'd found it.

THE END

EPILOGUE

This case is still considered open by the FBI and FAA.
It is unlikely that it will ever be solved.

ABOUT THE AUTHOR

Lorraine was born in Orlando, Florida. She won the title of Florida's Tangerine Queen, which earned her a modeling contract in New York. She was a model with the Ford Agency in New York in the 50's and 60's, posing for fashion and product ads, including television commercials. She is still a member of SAG, and now resides in Santa Monica, Ca. with her husband, writer Christopher Knopf. This is her first novel.

Proof

Made in the USA
Charleston, SC
17 December 2014